World-Building Harmony Setting Essentials

World-Building Harmony Setting Essentials

Rayan Musk

Noble Publishing

Contents

INDEX	1
Chapter 1	3
Chapter 2	19
Chapter 3	37
Chapter 4	52
Chapter 5	68
Chapter 6	83
Chapter 7	101
Chapter 8	116
Chapter 9	133

INDEX

Chapter 1: Introduction to World-Building
1.1 Define world-building and its importance in storytelling.
1.2 Discuss the impact of setting on a story's atmosphere and characters.
1.3 Explore the balance between creativity and coherence in world-building.

Chapter 2: Core Elements of Harmony Setting
2.1 Establish the concept of a "Harmony Setting" and its significance.
2.2 Delve into the interconnectedness of geography, climate, and ecosystems.
2.3 Introduce the idea that the setting itself has a character-like role in the narrative.

Chapter 3: Cultural Foundations
3.1 Explore how culture shapes the world and vice versa.
3.2 Discuss the influence of history, traditions, and belief systems on the setting.
3.3 Address the role of diverse cultures and their interactions in creating a harmonious world.

Chapter 4: Flora and Fauna
4.1 Examine the impact of unique plant and animal life on the setting.
4.2 Discuss how ecosystems contribute to the overall balance of the world.
4.3 Explore the symbiotic relationships between different species.

Chapter 5: Magic and Mysticism
5.1 Introduce supernatural elements and their role in the world.
5.2 Explore the rules of magic in the setting and its effects on the environment.
5.3 Discuss how mystical elements contribute to the harmony or disruption of the world.

Chapter 6: Architectural Wonders

6.1 Highlight the significance of architecture in world-building.
6.2 Explore how different civilizations shape their environments through buildings.
6.3 Discuss the impact of architectural choices on the overall harmony of the setting.

Chapter 7: Societal Harmony and Conflict
7.1 Examine social structures and their impact on the world.
7.2 Discuss how conflicts and resolutions contribute to the overall harmony.
7.3 Explore the role of societal dynamics in shaping the setting.

Chapter 8: Seasons and Cycles
8.1 Discuss the importance of seasonal changes in the setting.
8.2 Explore how natural cycles affect various aspects of the world.
8.3 Highlight the symbolism and impact of recurring patterns.

Chapter 9: Maintaining Harmony
9.1 Summarize key elements for creating and maintaining a harmonious setting.

9.2 Discuss how authors can ensure consistency and coherence throughout the narrative.

9.3 Explore potential challenges and solutions in maintaining harmony in the world-building process.

Chapter 1

Introduction to World-Building

World-building is an art that rises above the limits of writing, film, gaming, and different types of imaginative articulation. It is the specialty of making vivid and acceptable fictitious settings that act as the scenery for stories, undertakings, and encounters. Whether it's the rambling scenes of Center earth in J.R.R. Tolkien's "The Master of the Rings" or the tragic eventual fate of Margaret Atwood's "The Handmaid's Story," world-building is an essential part of narrating that enthralls crowds and transports them to new and fantastical domains.

At its center, world-building includes the careful development of a made up universe, complete with its own guidelines, societies, narratives, and geology. It is the establishment whereupon stories are fabricated, giving a rich embroidery to characters to possess and perusers or watchers to investigate. A very much created world can hoist a story from simple diversion to a completely vivid encounter, permitting crowds to suspend skepticism and become immersed in a fantastical reality.

One of the critical components of world-building is the foundation of a lucid and inside steady arrangement of decides and regulations that oversee the imaginary universe. These principles might relate to the actual laws of the world, like gravity, time, and space, or they might include enchanted or extraordinary components novel to the setting. For example, in the wizarding universe of J.K. Rowling's "Harry Potter" series, wizardry is a necessary piece of daily existence, with its own arrangement of spells, mixtures, and mysterious animals that stick to a particular mystical framework.

Topography assumes a critical part in molding the world and impacting the situation that transpire inside it. The actual scene, environment, and geology of a made up world can influence the characters' ways of life, societies, and, surprisingly, the actual plot. Think about the huge, cold breadth of Westeros in George R.R. Martin's "A Tune of Ice and Fire" series, where the unforgiving winters and flighty seasons add to the political interest and battles for control that characterize the story.

Societies inside a made up world are one more fundamental part of world-building. These societies are much of the time formed by the set of experiences, geology, and interesting elements of the world, bringing about different social orders with their own traditions, dialects, and social designs. Ursula K. Le Guin's "The Left Hand of Dimness" acquaints perusers with the hermaphroditic occupants of the planet Gethen, whose general public is affected by their capacity to change orientation voluntarily, testing regular ideas of character and cultural standards.

Besides, the historical backdrop of an imaginary world adds profundity and setting to the story, giving a feeling of progression and making sense of the present status of undertakings. Verifiable occasions, wars, and clashes shape the world and its occupants, leaving an enduring effect on the way of life and social orders that rise out of these encounters. Tolkien's Center earth, for instance, is saturated with a rich history of wars, unions, and the battle among great and fiendishness, as described in "The Silmarillion."

Notwithstanding the physical and social perspectives, the mechanical level of an imaginary world is an essential thought in world-building. The degree of innovative progression can go from crude social orders depending on enchantment or basic devices to cutting edge universes with cutting edge science and innovation. Philip K. Dick's "Do Androids Long for Electric Sheep?" imagines a tragic future where computerized reasoning and androids exist together with people, bringing up significant issues about character and cognizance.

Language, as well, assumes a critical part in world-building. Created dialects, or conlangs, add credibility to an imaginary world and add to the submersion of the crowd. J.R.R. Tolkien, a philologist himself, made elaborate dialects, for example, Elvish and Dwarvish for Center earth, improving the social embroidery of his reality and giving phonetic profundity to its different races.

World-building isn't restricted to writing; it stretches out its impact to the domains of film, TV, and gaming. In film, visual components like set plan, outfits, and embellishments add to the production of a conceivable and outwardly shocking world. Ridley Scott's "Sharp edge Sprinter" presents a coarse, modern Los Angeles with transcending high rises and neon-lit roads, laying out an outwardly striking cyberpunk stylish.

TV series like "Round of Privileged positions" exhibit the degree and intricacy of world-working in a serialized design. The show fastidiously rejuvenates the landmasses of Westeros and Essos, complete with particular societies, religions, and political plots. The complex world-building fills in as a scenery as well as turns into a basic piece of the story, impacting character inspirations and plot improvements.

The universe of gaming, especially in the class of pretending games (RPGs), depends vigorously on world-working to make sweeping and vivid gaming encounters. Games like "The Senior Parchments V: Skyrim" or "The Legend of Zelda: Breath of Nature" highlight immense open universes with different scenes, prisons, and non-player characters (NPCs). Players can investigate these universes, attempt missions, and drench themselves in the rich legend and history made by game designers.

The course of world-building is an exceptionally inventive and iterative one, frequently including cautious thought of different interconnected components. Creators, producers, and game engineers might begin with a focal idea or subject and slowly develop it, permitting the world to naturally advance. The degree of detail in world-building can fluctuate, from overgeneralized terms that give a general feeling of the world to minute subtleties that upgrade the authenticity and legitimacy of the setting.

Creators like Tolkien and Rowling are praised for their fastidious and far reaching world-building, making stories as well as whole folklores and chronicles for their made up universes. Tolkien, specifically, was known for his obligation to semantic and social subtleties, venturing to such an extreme as to make whole letter sets and schedules for his created dialects.

Conversely, a few works embrace a more moderate way to deal with world-building, leaving specific parts of the world purposely obscure or unexplained. This can make a feeling of secret and marvel, permitting the crowd to fill in the holes with their creative mind. It's a sensitive equilibrium, as an excess of detail can overpower, while too little can leave the crowd feeling disengaged from the world.

The impact of true societies, fantasies, and narratives on world-building is one more charming perspective to investigate. Many creators draw motivation from assorted sources, mixing components of various societies to make exceptional and dynamic fictitious universes.

Neil Gaiman's "American Divine beings" winds around together gods from different folklores, putting them in a contemporary American setting and investigating the crossing point of conviction and reality.

World-building likewise offers the potential chance to investigate social and political editorial inside the system of a made up story. Tragic universes, like those viewed as in Orwell's "1984" or Atwood's "The Handmaid's Story," act as wake up calls, utilizing overstated or speculative settings to resolve certifiable issues and cultural worries.

The gathering of world-building changes among crowds, for certain perusers or watchers attracted to complicated, broad universes, while others favor a more engaged and character-driven story. No matter what the methodology, powerful world-building improves the narrating experience by giving a rich and vivid scenery that supplements the characters and plot.

As innovation progresses, new mediums and stages offer inventive ways of drawing in with and experience fictitious universes. Computer generated reality (VR) and expanded reality (AR) advances, for instance, hold the possibility to change the manner in which crowds connect with and investigate fictitious settings. Envision venturing into the wizarding universe of Harry Potter through VR, where clients can meander through Diagon Rear entryway, go to classes at Hogwarts, or duel with sorcery in a completely vivid climate.

The cooperative idea of world-building is likewise obvious in fan networks that draw in with and develop existing fictitious universes. Fan fiction, fan craftsmanship, and online gatherings give stages to aficionados to contribute their own thoughts, understandings, and extensions of darling universes. This participatory part of world-building features the persevering through influence and social meaning of fictitious universes in the existences of fans.

In any case, world-building isn't without its difficulties and possible entanglements. The gamble of irregularity or inconsistency inside the laid out rules of an imaginary world is a steady concern. Creators and makers should keep a harmony among inventiveness and lucidness, guaranteeing that the different components of the world line up with one another and add to a brought together and convincing entirety.

Moreover, the compulsion to focus on world-working to the detriment of character improvement or story pacing is a typical entanglement. While a lavishly nitty gritty world can enthrall crowds, the characters and their processes structure the profound center of any story. Finding some kind of harmony between world-building and narrating is fundamental to making a convincing and balanced story.

All in all, world-building is a complex and dynamic part of narrating that rises above kinds and mediums. Whether in writing, film, TV, or gaming, the making of fictitious universes considers boundless imagination and investigation. From the huge scenes of epic dream to the modern cityscapes of sci-fi, world-building fills in as the material whereupon stories show some major signs of life.

1.1 Define world-building and its importance in storytelling.

World-building is a fundamental and complex part of narrating that includes the making of vivid and convincing fictitious universes. It envelops the improvement of definite settings, societies, chronicles, and decides that oversee the imaginary world wherein a story unfurls. This scholarly and imaginative procedure isn't restricted to a particular type and tracks down application in writing, film, TV, gaming, and different types of creative articulation. The significance of world-building lies in its capacity to upgrade the in general narrating experience by giving a rich and charming background for characters and occasions.

At its quintessence, world-building goes past the simple depiction of actual scenes; it includes the development of a rational and inside reliable climate with its own remarkable qualities. These attributes can go from the laws of physical science and geology to the presence of enchantment or cutting edge innovation, contingent upon the class and account prerequisites. A definitive objective of world-building is to ship crowds to a world that feels genuine, charming them in an other reality where they can suspend mistrust and completely draw in with the story.

One of the essential elements of world-building is to lay out a bunch of decides or regulations that oversee the made up universe. These guidelines make a structure inside which the characters and occasions work, adding a layer of authenticity and lucidness to the story. Whether it's the enchanted framework in a dream domain or the cutting edge innovation in a sci-fi setting, these guidelines give a feeling of request and consistency that adds to the general trustworthiness of the world. This consistency is significant for crowd submersion, as deviations from laid out rules can upset the account stream and debilitate the association between the crowd and the story.

Geology assumes a urgent part in world-building, impacting the actual parts of the setting as well as the characters' ways of life, societies, and connections. The geology, environment, and normal highlights of a made up world shape the encounters of its occupants, setting out special difficulties and open doors. Think about the effect of the cruel winters in George R.R. Martin's "A Tune of Ice and Fire," where the approaching danger of winter turns into a main thrust behind political interest and battles for control. The topography of a world fills in as something other than a background; it turns into a functioning member in forming the story.

Social variety inside a made up world is one more basic component of world-building. Societies are formed by the set of experiences, geology, and remarkable elements of the world, prompting an embroidery of social orders with unmistakable traditions, dialects, and social designs.

Ursula K. Le Guin's "The Left Hand of Obscurity" investigates a reality where occupants can change orientation voluntarily, testing ordinary cultural standards and impression of character. The variety of societies adds profundity and intricacy to the world, enhancing the story with various viewpoints and encounters.

The historical backdrop of an imaginary world fills in as an establishment for the story, making sense of the present status of undertakings and giving setting to the characters' activities. Verifiable occasions, wars, and clashes leave an enduring effect on the way of life and social orders inside the world, molding their convictions, values, and connections. J.R.R. Tolkien's Center earth, as itemized in "The Silmarillion," is saturated with a rich history of wars, partnerships, and the timeless battle among great and malevolence. The verifiable profundity adds layers to the narrating, making a feeling of profundity and coherence that resounds with crowds.

Mechanical level is one more imperative part of world-building, deciding the degree of headway in science, innovation, and development inside the made up universe. This can go from crude social orders depending on wizardry or basic devices to modern universes with cutting edge advanced mechanics and computerized reasoning. Philip K. Dick's "Do Androids Long for Electric Sheep?" imagines a tragic future where man-made reasoning and androids coincide with people, investigating significant inquiries regarding character and cognizance. The innovative scene impacts the characters' regular routines as well as the all-encompassing topics and clashes inside the account.

Language, as well, assumes an essential part in world-building. Designed dialects, known as conlangs, add to the validness of a made up world, offering a one of a kind phonetic personality to its occupants. J.R.R. Tolkien, a philologist, created elaborate dialects, for example, Elvish and Dwarvish for Center earth, improving the social extravagance of his reality. Language isn't simply an instrument for correspondence; it turns into a social relic, mirroring the set of experiences and personality of the social orders inside the made up world.

World-building isn't restricted to writing; its impact stretches out to film, TV, and gaming. In film, visual components like set plan, outfits, and enhancements add to the formation of a credible and outwardly shocking world. Ridley Scott's "Sharp edge

Sprinter" gives a tragic future transcending high rises and neon-lit roads, laying out an outwardly striking cyberpunk stylish. TV series like "Round of Privileged positions" exhibit the extension and intricacy of world-working in a serialized design, where the complexities of societies and political scenes become vital to the story.

Gaming, especially in the class of pretending games (RPGs), vigorously depends on world-working to make far reaching and vivid gaming encounters. Games like "The Senior Parchments V: Skyrim" or "The Legend of Zelda: Breath of Nature" highlight tremendous open universes with different scenes, prisons, and non-player characters (NPCs).

Players can investigate these universes, attempt missions, and drench themselves in the rich legend and history created by game designers. The intuitive idea of gaming takes into consideration a more straightforward and participatory commitment with the imaginary universe.

The course of world-building is a profoundly imaginative and iterative one, frequently including the continuous development of a focal idea or subject. Makers might begin with a center thought and dynamically add layers of detail, permitting the world to naturally develop. The degree of detail in world-building can change, from overgeneralized terms that give a general feeling of the world to minute subtleties that upgrade the authenticity and genuineness of the setting. Creators, movie producers, and game engineers explore the fragile harmony between giving sufficient detail to dazzle crowds and leaving space for creative mind and translation.

A few makers, as J.R.R. Tolkien and J.K. Rowling, are praised for their fastidious and extensive world-building. These creators made convincing accounts as well as evolved whole legends, dialects, and narratives for their imaginary universes. Tolkien, specifically, was known for his obligation to etymological and social subtleties, making an immense and interconnected world that rose above the story of "The Ruler of the Rings."

Contrastingly, a few works embrace a more moderate way to deal with world-building, leaving specific perspectives purposely unclear or unexplained. This moderate methodology considers a feeling of secret and marvel, welcoming crowds to fill in the holes with their creative mind. It is a sensitive equilibrium, as a lot of detail can overpower, while too little can leave the crowd feeling detached from the world.

The impact of certifiable societies, fantasies, and accounts on world-building is an interesting perspective to investigate. Numerous makers draw motivation from assorted sources, mixing components of various societies to make one of a kind and energetic fictitious universes. Neil Gaiman's "American Divine beings" winds around together divinities from different legends, putting them in a contemporary American setting and investigating the crossing point of conviction and reality. This exchange between the fantastical and the recognizable adds layers of significance to the account, welcoming crowds to ponder their own social convictions and practices.

World-building likewise gives the potential chance to investigate social and political critique inside the system of a made up story. Tragic universes, like those viewed as in

Orwell's "1984" or Atwood's "The Handmaid's Story," act as wake up calls, utilizing overstated or speculative settings to resolve certifiable issues and cultural worries. By introducing elective real factors, makers can provoke crowds to consider the ramifications of specific belief systems or ways of behaving.

The gathering of world-building shifts among crowds, for certain perusers or watchers attracted to many-sided, sweeping universes, while others favor a more engaged and character-driven story. No matter what the methodology, powerful world-building upgrades the narrating experience by giving a rich and vivid background that supplements the characters and plot. It makes a feeling of spot and time, welcoming crowds to investigate and put sincerely in the imaginary universe.

As innovation propels, new mediums and stages offer imaginative ways of drawing in with and experience fictitious universes. Computer generated reality (VR) and increased reality (AR) advancements, for instance, hold the possibility to upset the manner in which crowds collaborate with and investigate fictitious settings. Envision venturing into the wizarding universe of Harry Potter through VR, where clients can meander through Diagon Back street, go to classes at Hogwarts, or duel with enchantment in a completely vivid climate. These arising advancements can possibly reclassify crowd commitment, giving uncommon degrees of drenching and intuitiveness.

1.2 Discuss the impact of setting on a story's atmosphere and characters.

The setting of a story fills in as a strong and diverse component that essentially impacts the environment and characters inside a story. It is something beyond a background; the setting shapes the mind-set, tone, and generally speaking vibe of the story, making a setting that can improve or oblige the unfurling occasions. Furthermore, the climate in what characters exist frequently assumes a significant part in molding their characters, inspirations, and cooperations. By digging into the multifaceted connection between setting, environment, and characters, we can acquire a more profound comprehension of how these components merge to make convincing and vivid stories.

Most importantly, the setting lays out the establishment for the climate of a story. Whether it's a rambling city, a barren wild, or an interesting town, the physical and natural credits of the setting add to the general state of mind of the story. Consider, for example, the dim and agonizing climate of Victorian-time London in Bram Stoker's "Dracula." The haze loaded roads, forcing engineering, and strange rear entryways all add to a feeling of premonition and disquiet, uplifting the tension and gothic components of the story.

Conversely, the splendid and unspoiled setting of a radiant ocean side town in a transitioning novel could summon sensations of wistfulness, warmth, and idealism. The tactile subtleties of the setting — like the fragrance of the ocean, the sound of seagulls, or the vibe of sand between toes — add to a clear and vivid environment that supplements the subjects and feelings of the story. The setting turns into a powerful power that shapes the profound scene of the story, impacting how perusers see and interface with the characters and occasions.

Besides, the time span in which a story is set can significantly influence its climate. Verifiable settings, for instance, convey with them the social, social, and political subtleties of a particular period. The Victorian Britain of Charles Dickens' books mirrors the cultural variations and modern difficulties of the time, making a scenery that educates the battles and yearnings regarding the characters. Essentially, a story set in the Thundering Twenties with its jazz-filled speakeasies and post-war bafflement would bring out an immensely unexpected air in comparison to one set in the cutting edge, mechanically progressed scene of a cyberpunk world.

The actual qualities of the setting, like weather patterns, likewise assume an essential part in forming air. A turbulent night can uplift strain and make a feeling of looming struggle, as seen in numerous gothic and thrilling stories. Then again, a peaceful and sunlit day might imbue a story with a feeling of serenity, making way for snapshots of thoughtfulness or disclosure. The interaction between the normal components and the occasions of the story adds layers of intricacy to the general air, upgrading the profound effect on the two characters and perusers.

Past environment, the setting fundamentally impacts the characters possessing the account. Characters are not disconnected elements; they exist inside the setting of their environmental elements, and the climate shape their encounters, ways of behaving, and perspectives. The socio-social parts of the setting, including its standards, values, and customs, add to the improvement of characters and their connections.

Consider a story set in a closely knit local area where everybody knows one another's business. The characters, impacted by the public idea of their current circumstance, may wrestle with issues of similarity, cultural assumptions, or the battle for uniqueness inside an aggregate personality. Then again, characters in a rambling metropolitan scene could explore the difficulties of namelessness, disengagement, and the journey for association in a clamoring and generic world. In the two cases, the setting turns into a unique power molding the characters' personalities and impacting the directions of their curves.

The financial and geological parts of the setting additionally influence characters' lives and yearnings. A story set in a tragic future where assets are scant could portray characters battling for endurance in a brutal and unforgiving climate. Their inspirations might spin around essential requirements like food, sanctuary, and security, making a story zeroed in on versatility and genius. Conversely, characters in a special, princely setting might wrestle with existential inquiries, individual satisfaction, or the results of cultural assumptions.

Besides, the setting can act as an emblematic background that mirrors or differences with the characters' subtle conflicts. In F. Scott Fitzgerald's "The Incomparable Gatsby," the rich chateaus and wanton gatherings of the Jazz Age act as a sparkling exterior that veils the characters' basic disappointment and moral rot.

The distinct dissimilarity between the outward luxury and the characters' unseen struggles adds profundity to the story, involving the setting as a figurative focal point through which to investigate subjects of riches, class, and the Pursuit of happiness.

As well as affecting person advancement, the setting can shape character connections and cooperations. A restricted and claustrophobic setting, like a spaceship in a sci-fi spine chiller, may escalate the elements between characters, prompting uplifted strain and clashes. Then again, a rustic and quiet setting, similar to an unassuming community in a romance book, may work with cozy associations and cultivate a feeling of local area among characters.

The setting likewise assumes a vital part in deciding characters' occupations, ways of life, and everyday schedules. A person living in a clamoring metropolitan focus might have a quick moving, requesting position that mirrors the cutthroat and aggressive nature of the climate. Contrastingly, a person in a provincial setting might participate in agrarian exercises, underlining an association with nature and a more slow, more scrutinizing lifestyle. These subtleties not just add to the validness of the characters yet additionally highlight the harmonious connection among characters and their environmental factors.

Besides, the setting can go about as an impetus for character struggle and development. Setting characters in testing or new conditions drives them to face impediments, pursue hard decisions, and go through private changes. In Joseph Conrad's "Heart of Obscurity," the deceptive and secretive setting of the Congo Waterway turns into a cauldron for the hero, Marlow, as he wrestles with the haziness inside himself and the ethical intricacies of imperialism. The brutal and unforgiving setting turns into a mirror that reflects and enhances the characters' conflicts under the surface.

The effect of setting on characters reaches out to the account's plot and subjects. The setting can direct the potential outcomes and limitations inside which the story unfurls. A story set in a dystopian no man's land, for instance, may investigate topics of endurance, strength, and the results of natural debasement. The setting turns into an indispensable piece of the story's topical structure, impacting the struggles, predicaments, and goals that the characters face.

Think about the exemplary book "To Kill a Mockingbird" by Harper Lee, set in the racially charged air of the American South during the 1930s. The setting, pervaded by profoundly instilled racial biases and social pecking orders, turns into a cauldron for the characters to wrestle with issues of equity, ethical quality, and compassion. The account's investigation of racial treachery is complicatedly attached to the authentic and social setting of the Southern setting, highlighting the significant effect of the climate on both plot and subject.

1.3 Explore the balance between creativity and coherence in world-building.

World-building is an unpredictable art that includes the production of fictitious universes, each with its own arrangement of rules, societies, accounts, and scenes. One of the essential difficulties in world-building is finding some kind of harmony among imagination and lucidness. While the inventive flow takes into consideration limitless creative mind and development, lucidness guarantees that the different components of the world line up with one another, making a bound together and conceivable entirety. This equilibrium is essential for the outcome of a made up universe, whether it exists in writing, film, TV, or gaming.

At its center, innovativeness in world-building includes the creative investigation of novel thoughts, ideas, and conceivable outcomes. Makers leave on an excursion of innovation, splitting away from the requirements of reality to create settings that spellbind crowds with their uniqueness and creativity. In writing, visionaries like J.R.R. Tolkien and J.K. Rowling have set the bar high for inventive world-building, acquainting perusers with unpredictably point by point domains like Center earth and the wizarding scene. These universes are not simple impressions of our own; they are inventive scenes with their own arrangement of rules and ponders.

Nonetheless, the limitless idea of imagination presents a test in keeping up with rationality inside the world. Without a feeling of inside consistency, a made up universe might risk losing its vivid power. Muddled components can disturb the willingness to accept some far-fetched situations, reducing the crowd's capacity to put resources into the story. Thusly, the test for world-manufacturers is to channel their imaginative motivations into a system that guarantees sensible associations between various features of the world.

Think about the enchanted framework in J.K. Rowling's Harry Potter series. While the world is wealthy in mystical components, Rowling lays out a cognizant supernatural framework with rules and restrictions. Spells have chants and explicit wand developments, mystical animals stick to their own science and conduct, and there are ramifications to the abuse of sorcery. This rationality grounds the enchanted components, causing them to feel like an indispensable and authentic piece of the wizarding scene.

The geological and social parts of an imaginary world are similarly dependent upon the harmony among imagination and lucidness. The scenes, environments, and geography should line up with the laid out rules and subjects of the world. In Tolkien's Center earth, the assorted scenes — from the charming Shire to the misleading Mordor — reflect the more extensive subjects of the account, upgrading the soundness of the world. The way of life inside Center earth, each with its own dialects, narratives, and customs, add to the profundity and extravagance of the world while sticking to a steady interior rationale.

In the domain of film, visual cognizance is especially urgent. The tasteful decisions, including set plan, ensembles, and cinematography, should line up with the laid out world-building components to make an outwardly durable encounter. Ridley Scott's "Edge Sprinter" represents this equilibrium, introducing a cyberpunk vision representing things to come where each visual component adds to the general air and subjects of the story. The neon-lit roads, transcending high rises, and downpour drenched climate blend to shape an outwardly intelligible and vivid world.

The mechanical level of a made up world is one more viewpoint that requests cautious thought yet to be determined among inventiveness and cognizance. Whether it's a steampunk world with Victorian-time innovation controlled by steam, a spacefaring development with cutting edge interstellar travel, or a tragic future with robotic improvements, the mechanical perspectives should line up with the general vision of the world. Philip K. Dick's "Do Androids Long for Electric Sheep?" imagines a future where androids are unclear from people, bringing up issues about the idea of cognizance and character. The innovative components, while imaginative, fill an intelligent topical need inside the story.

Language, as well, assumes an essential part in world-building, and the formation of designed dialects, or conlangs, is a demonstration of the imaginative capability of etymological components. J.R.R. Tolkien's dialects, for example, Elvish and Dwarvish, add to the credibility and social lavishness of Center earth. In any case, these dialects are not erratic; they observe etymological guidelines and designs, exhibiting Tolkien's obligation to soundness even in the littlest subtleties of his reality.

The verifiable setting and course of events of an imaginary world give another aspect where innovativeness and soundness converge. The occasions that shape the historical backdrop of the world should line up with the laid out rules and topics, making a feeling of coherence and rationale. George R.R. Martin's "A Tune of Ice and Fire" series, adjusted into the TV series "Round of Lofty positions," presents an intricate trap of political interest and epic showdowns across numerous locales. The authentic occasions, like Robert's Insubordination and the Targaryen triumph, are complicatedly woven into the account, adding to the soundness of the world and the inspirations of its characters.

Be that as it may, the test of adjusting imagination and rationality stretches out past individual components to the general tone and environment of the world. A world that is too fantastical or detached may battle to connect with crowds inwardly, while a world that is too unbending or commonplace might neglect to catch their creative mind. The overall subjects and tone should reverberate with the innovative vision while keeping up with inside consistency.

Creators and makers frequently wrestle with the compulsion to over-burden their universes with unreasonable detail, accepting that greater intricacy compares to a more extravagant encounter. While detail is fundamental, an overabundance of data can overpower crowds and reduce the center account.

Ursula K. Le Guin's "The Left Hand of Haziness" is a masterclass in adjusting subtlety and story center. The universe of Gethen, with its gender ambiguous occupants and exceptional cultural designs, is given sufficient detail to improve the story however not such a lot of that it diverts from the focal subjects of the account.

Moreover, the harmony among imagination and rationality is obvious in the treatment of social components inside an imaginary world. Social variety adds profundity and genuineness, yet the joining of social components should be finished with responsiveness and reason. Drawing motivation from genuine societies can add to a more nuanced and engaging fictitious world. Nonetheless, social allocation or conflicting portrayal can subvert the lucidness of the world and sustain destructive generalizations.

Neil Gaiman's "American Divine beings" explores this equilibrium by integrating gods from different folklores into a contemporary American setting. The social variety turns into a topical investigation of conviction frameworks and cultural movements, adding to the intelligence of the story while embracing the imaginative combination of folklores.

In the domain of gaming, where player cooperation and organization are foremost, the test of adjusting imagination and soundness turns out to be significantly more complicated. Pretending games (RPGs) frequently highlight open universes with far reaching legend and incalculable intelligent components. Games like "The Senior Parchments V: Skyrim" prevail by giving an immense and nitty gritty world for players to investigate while keeping up with inside consistency. The different groups, races, and scenes add to the vivid experience without overpowering players with muddled data.

The cooperative idea of world-working, as found in fan networks and expanded universes, adds an extra layer of intricacy to the harmony among imagination and rationality. Fan fiction, craftsmanship, and conversations add to the developing story of a made up world. Makers should explore the convergence of innovative commitments while keeping up with command over the center components that characterize the world. The "Star Wars" extended universe, for instance, has seen a huge range of innovative commitments from fans, however official ordinance is cautiously organized to save the intelligence of the bigger story.

Nonetheless, the strain among imagination and rationality is certainly not a static balance; a powerful cycle requires continuous thought and transformation. As accounts develop and grow, makers should reconsider the lucidness of their universes and change components in like manner. The presentation of new characters, occasions, or settings ought to upgrade the general account without sabotaging the laid out rules and subjects.

The traps of world-working without a harmony among imagination and lucidness are obvious in occurrences where makers focus on display over substance. Conflicting guidelines, erratic changes, or the presentation of components exclusively for shock worth can disintegrate the uprightness of the world and withdraw crowds.

The last time of "Round of Privileged positions" got analysis for saw slips in rationality, for certain watchers communicating disappointment with character curves and plot improvements that seemed to digress from laid out designs.

Likewise, the test of keeping up with lucidness is available in shared realistic universes, where numerous makers add to a firm story across various movies and characters. The Wonder Realistic Universe (MCU) is a remarkable illustration of effective world-working across different movies and characters. Every portion adds with the overall account while complying to the laid out rules of the universe. The harmony between imaginative independence for individual movie producers and adherence to a strong vision requires cautious coordination and correspondence.

Soundness in world-building is a basic viewpoint that guarantees the consistent reconciliation of different components inside a made up universe. While innovativeness considers the investigation of clever thoughts, lucidness gives the structure important to these plans to shape a bound together and reasonable entirety. Accomplishing a sensitive harmony among imagination and cognizance is vital, as it straightforwardly impacts the viability of an imaginary world in writing, film, TV, and gaming.

The rationality of an imaginary world envelops inner consistency, coherent associations between various parts, and a feeling of trustworthiness. Without intelligibility, a world dangers feeling disconnected, impossible, and unfit to support the willingness to accept some far-fetched situations fundamental for crowd inundation. Thusly, world-developers should explore the multifaceted test of keeping a firm story while embracing the endless open doors for imagination.

The idea of intelligence reaches out to different components of world-building, beginning with the foundation of decides and regulations that oversee the imaginary universe. Whether it includes enchanted frameworks, trend setting innovation, or the laws of physical science, these principles make a system inside what characters and occasions work. Ursula K. Le Guin's "Earthsea" series epitomizes this soundness by presenting an enchanted framework with obviously characterized rules and results. The consistency of the mysterious components adds to the vivid nature of the world, supporting that enchantment is an essential and intelligible piece of the Earthsea universe.

Geology, environment, and geography likewise assume crucial parts in molding the rationality of an imaginary world. The actual qualities of the setting should line up with the laid out rules and subjects, establishing an amicable connection between the climate and the story. J.R.R. Tolkien's Center earth is a masterclass in such manner, where the different scenes — from the peaceful Shire to the premonition Mordor — mirror the more extensive subjects of the story. The intelligence between the actual world and the general story enhances the vivid experience for perusers.

Social components inside an imaginary world, including dialects, customs, and cultural designs, contribute essentially to soundness. By laying out steady social standards, world-manufacturers upgrade the legitimacy of their universes and give a sensible setting to character ways of behaving. In the "Ridge" series by Blunt Herbert, the complicated social and political designs of the different groups add to the soundness of the universe. The communications between characters are grounded in the laid out social setting, adding profundity and authenticity to the story.

Keeping up with cognizance in the verifiable setting and timetable of a made up world is similarly urgent. The occasions that shape the world's set of experiences should line up with the laid out rules and topics, making a feeling of coherence and rationale. George R.R. Martin's "A Melody of Ice and Fire" series, adjusted into the TV series "Round of Privileged positions," flawlessly meshes verifiable occasions like Robert's Insubordination into the story texture. The soundness of the world's set of experiences enhances character inspirations and plot improvements, establishing them in a context oriented system.

The harmony among imagination and soundness is especially clear in the treatment of innovation inside a made up world. Whether it's a cutting edge society with cutting edge advanced mechanics or a steampunk world with Victorian-time innovation, the innovative components should line up with the general vision of the world. Philip K. Dick's "Do Androids Long for Electric Sheep?" investigates a future where androids are vague from people, presenting mechanical components that fill a reasonable topical need inside the story.

Language, as well, adds to the intelligence of an imaginary world, particularly when makers create designed dialects, known as conlangs. J.R.R. Tolkien's dialects, for example, Elvish and Dwarvish, add extravagance with Center earth as well as comply to etymological standards and designs. This obligation to rationality, even in semantic subtleties, highlights the careful world-building that upgrades the general trustworthiness of the setting.

Visual soundness is especially vital in film, where the stylish decisions, including set plan, ensembles, and cinematography, should line up with the laid out world-building components. Ridley Scott's "Cutting edge Sprinter" presents a cyberpunk vision representing things to come where each visual component adds to the general climate and subjects of the story. The neon-lit roads, transcending high rises, and downpour doused climate blend to shape an outwardly intelligent and vivid world.

The harmony among innovativeness and intelligibility stretches out to the treatment of verifiable and social components inside a made up world. Drawing motivation from certifiable societies can add to a more nuanced and interesting fictitious world. Be that as it may, social apportionment or conflicting portrayal can subvert the cognizance of the world and propagate destructive generalizations.

Neil Gaiman's "American Divine beings" explores this equilibrium by integrating divinities from different legends into a contemporary American setting. The social variety turns into a topical investigation of conviction frameworks and cultural movements, adding to the rationality of the story while embracing the innovative combination of folklores.

In the domain of gaming, keeping up with cognizance is especially difficult because of the intelligent idea of the medium. Pretending games (RPGs) frequently include open universes with sweeping legend and endless intuitive components. Games like "The Senior Parchments V: Skyrim" prevail by giving a tremendous and point by point world for players to investigate while keeping up with inside consistency. The different groups, races, and scenes add to the vivid experience without overpowering players with garbled data.

The cooperative idea of world-working, as found in fan networks and expanded universes, adds an extra layer of intricacy to the harmony among imagination and lucidness. Fan fiction, workmanship, and conversations add to the developing story of a made up world. Makers should explore the inundation of innovative commitments while keeping up with command over the center components that characterize the world. The "Star Wars" extended universe, for instance, has seen an immense range of innovative commitments from fans, yet official ordinance is cautiously organized to save the intelligibility of the bigger story.

Nonetheless, the pressure among inventiveness and rationality is certainly not a static balance; a unique interaction requires progressing thought and variation. As accounts advance and grow, makers should reevaluate the intelligibility of their universes and change components in like manner. The presentation of new characters, occasions, or settings ought to improve the general account without sabotaging the laid out rules and subjects.

The traps of world-working without a harmony among imagination and lucidness are clear in examples where makers focus on exhibition over substance. Conflicting guidelines, erratic changes, or the presentation of components exclusively for shock worth can dissolve the respectability of the world and withdraw crowds. The last time of "Round of High positions" got analysis for saw slips in cognizance, for certain watchers communicating disappointment with character bends and plot improvements that seemed to veer off from laid out designs.

Likewise, the test of keeping up with rationality is available in shared true to life universes, where various makers add to a durable story across various movies and characters. The Wonder Realistic Universe (MCU) is a prominent illustration of fruitful world-working across numerous movies and characters. Every portion adds with the overall story while complying to the laid out rules of the universe. The harmony between inventive independence for individual movie producers and adherence to a firm vision requires cautious coordination and correspondence.

At last, the effective harmony among imagination and rationality in world-building is a demonstration of the expertise and vision of the makers. It includes a nuanced comprehension of the topical, stylish, and story components that characterize the world. The interaction requires a readiness to investigate groundbreaking thoughts while keeping a pledge to inside consistency.

All in all, rationality in world-building is a dynamic and diverse undertaking that requests a sensitive balance among imagination and adherence to laid out rules. The inventive flow takes into consideration the investigation of novel thoughts, ideas, and potential outcomes, leading to fictitious universes that enrapture crowds with their innovation and profundity. Nonetheless, intelligence is similarly indispensable, guaranteeing that the different components of the world line up with one another to make a brought together and conceivable entirety.

Creators, movie producers, and game designers explore this equilibrium across assorted mediums, from writing to film to gaming. The effective reconciliation of imagination and lucidness upgrades the narrating experience, drenching crowds in universes that resound with validness and charm the creative mind. The continuous development of world-building, prodded by propels in innovation and the cooperative endeavors of makers and fans, holds energizing possibilities for what's to come. However long the sensitive equilibrium is kept up with, fictitious universes will keep on being ripe justification for investigation, disclosure, and the vast conceivable outcomes of the human creative mind.

Chapter 2

Core Elements of Harmony Setting

In the immense territory of the universe, settled inside the enormous embroidery of presence, there exists a domain known as Concordance. This ethereal aspect isn't limited by the laws of the actual world, yet rather, it flourishes with the immaterial strings that wind through the texture of feelings, associations, and the embodiment of being. The Center Components of Concordance, crucial powers that oversee this domain, act as the support points supporting the sensitive equilibrium that supports all of presence inside this otherworldly space.

At the core of Agreement lies the principal center component, Solidarity. The power ties each bit of energy, each conscious being, and each theoretical idea into a firm entirety. Solidarity rises above the limits of independence and encourages a shared mindset that reverberates all through the domain. The orchestra blends the different voices of the universe, considering an intermingling of energies and thoughts that shape the actual groundwork of Concordance.

Inverse yet corresponding to Solidarity is Variety, the second center component. While Solidarity ties, Variety extends the skyline of conceivable outcomes. It is the festival of contrasts, the acknowledgment of special characteristics that every element brings to the vast woven artwork. Variety is the flash that touches off innovativeness, cultivating the development and advancement of the domain. It appears in the horde types of life, each with its own story and reason, adding to the fantastic account of Congruity.

The third center component is Harmony, the sensitive equilibrium that guarantees neither Solidarity nor Variety overpowers the other. The astronomical balance keeps turmoil from destroying the texture of Congruity. Balance appears in the repeating idea of presence, the recurring pattern of energies that keep everything under control and forestall stagnation. The power directs the domain through the dance of creation and obliteration, taking into consideration reestablishment and development.

Associated personally to Balance is Reverberation, the fourth center component. Reverberation is the reverberation of activities and feelings that resounds across the embroidery of Concordance. It is the expanding influence that impacts the course of occasions, making associations that rise above existence. Reverberation ties elements together, making bonds that persevere through difficulties and wins. The inconspicuous string winds around the complex examples of predetermination.

The fifth center component, Quietness, pervades each edge of Agreement with serenity and harmony. It is the quietness inside the confusion, the quiet that wins even despite affliction. Tranquility is the analgesic that mitigates the injuries of presence, permitting substances to track down comfort and reflection. The delicate murmur directs the domain towards internal concordance, cultivating a feeling of equilibrium and prosperity.

As Amicability winds around its multifaceted dance, the 6th center component, Progress, pushes the domain forward. The power of progress drives development and development. Progress is the always consistent movement that pushes substances to investigate new wildernesses, to enhance, and to look for higher comprehension. The impetus changes the domain, guaranteeing that stagnation respects the persistent walk of time.

The seventh and last center component, Sympathy, is the scaffold that interfaces the different strings of Congruity. It is the capacity to comprehend and discuss the thoughts of others, encouraging a profound feeling of association. Sympathy is the power that ties substances in empathy, permitting them to explore the intricacies of associations with understanding and generosity. The wellspring of aggregate inclination supports the solidarity of the domain.

Inside this grandiose artful dance of center components, substances as one track down their motivation and importance. Solidarity, Variety, Harmony, Reverberation, Serenity, Progress, and Sympathy entwine in an amicable dance, making an orchestra of presence that resounds
through the actual texture of the domain. Each center component assumes an imperative part, and their transaction characterizes the pith of life in this ethereal aspect.

The setting of Agreement isn't bound to actual scenes or divine bodies; rather, it rises above the customary ideas of reality. It is a domain formed by the connections of conscious creatures, energy flows, and the consistently present impact of the center components. Substances together as one are not limited by bodily structures; all things being equal, they exist as appearances of energy and cognizance, formed and impacted by the center components that oversee their reality.

In the domain of Amicability, there are no particular limits between oneself and the other. Substances are interconnected, their energies joined in a mind boggling embroidery that mirrors the shared perspective of the domain. The texture of Amicability is always showing signs of change, answering the recurring pattern of feelings, contemplations, and activities. It is a unique material whereupon the tales of presence are painted.

The scene of Congruity is an impression of the center components at play. Tremendous breadths of ethereal energy dance in designs that reflect the balance and progress of the domain. Colors shift and mix, addressing the variety that characterizes the pith of Congruity. Heaps of peacefulness ascend in quiet grandness, and waterways of reverberation move through the scene, conveying the reverberations of past activities.

Occupants of Concordance are creatures of energy and awareness, molded by the center components that resound inside them. They exist in a condition of consistent motion, developing and adjusting in light of the steadily changing flows of the domain. Connections among elements are fashioned through empathic associations, and the bonds they make reverberation in the shared mindset of Congruity.

The pattern of presence together as one is portrayed by the exchange of creation and disintegration. Substances are brought into the world from the energies of the domain, their quintessence formed by the center components that impact their being. As they navigate the grandiose dance, encountering the ups and downs of presence, they add to the continuous account of Congruity. At last, substances return to the energy pool, their pith converging with the shared perspective.

Time together as one isn't direct however repeating, reflecting the everlasting dance of the center components. Elements experience snapshots of presence, each adding to the consistently extending embroidery of the domain. The past, present, and future are entwined, and the reverberations of activities wait in the reverberation of the shared perspective. It is an immortal domain where the idea of "for eternity" takes on a significant and ever-present importance.

The infinite powers that oversee Concordance are not unchanging; they answer the activities and selections of substances. The equilibrium of the center components can be tipped, prompting times of disunity and choppiness. In such occasions, the domain encounters commotion as substances wrestle with the outcomes of their aggregate activities. However, the innate versatility of Concordance guarantees that, through contemplation and understanding, balance is ultimately reestablished.

Substances as one have the capacity to control the center components somewhat. This control isn't an activity of control but instead an agreeable joint effort with the powers that shape their reality. The gifted professionals of basic control can channel the energies of Solidarity, bridle the innovative force of Variety, keep up with the sensitive equilibrium of Harmony, and tap into the full flows that interface all substances.

Mysterious safe-havens and areas exist inside the scene of Concordance, where substances assemble to investigate the more profound secrets of the center components. These safe-havens act as central focuses for thoughtfulness, learning, and fellowship. The insightful elderly folks and guides inside these territories offer direction to those looking for a more profound comprehension of the inestimable powers that shape their reality.

Ventures together as one are not actual campaigns but rather otherworldly odysseys. Substances leave on journeys of self-disclosure, looking to conform to the amicable progression of the center components. These excursions might take them to the most distant spans of the ethereal scene or profound inside the openings of their own cognizance. Each journey is a journey toward illumination, a mission to fit with the key powers that oversee their reality.

The occupants of Amicability are not invulnerable to struggle, as the interchange of center components once in a while prompts dissension. In the midst of lopsidedness, substances might confront difficulties that test how they might interpret the center components and their capacity to explore the many-sided dance of presence. However, misfortune together as one isn't a harbinger of destruction yet a chance for development and change.

The vast woven artwork of Amicability isn't static however steadily developing. Elements, through their activities and decisions, add to the continuous story of the domain. As they navigate the grandiose dance, they leave engraves on the shared awareness, forming the fate of Concordance. The accounts of affection, hardship, win, and misfortune become strings in the fantastic embroidered artwork, each adding to the rich and multifaceted story of the domain.

In the domain of Concordance, elements coincide in a sensitive equilibrium of interconnectedness. The shared mindset ties them together, cultivating a feeling of solidarity that rises above distinction.

Sympathy fills in as the scaffold that permits elements to comprehend and partake in the encounters of others, making a trap of associations that enhance the texture of presence. In this interconnected embroidered artwork, the prosperity of one is personally attached to the prosperity of all.

Congruity isn't a perfect world absent any and all difficulties, yet rather a domain where substances explore the intricacies of presence with a comprehension of the center components. The infinite dance proceeds, and elements figure out how to orchestrate with the recurring pattern of energies that shape their world. In the midst of conflict.

2.1 Establish the concept of a "Harmony Setting" and its significance.

The idea of a "Congruity Setting" addresses an exceptional and vivid account system, rising above regular thoughts of narrating. A setting goes past the physical and transient, digging into the magical and inestimable parts of presence. As one Setting, the central powers that oversee the universe are exemplified and given organization, making a dynamic and interconnected domain where the actual texture of the truth is molded by these enormous components.

At its center, the Concordance Setting is described by the presence of center components that characterize and impact the idea of the setting. These center components, like Solidarity, Variety, Balance, Reverberation, Peacefulness, Progress, and Sympathy, are not only dynamic ideas but rather no nonsense powers that oversee the back and forth movement of presence inside the setting. Every component assumes an essential part, joining with the others to make a rich and complex embroidery of vast powers.

The meaning of the Congruity Setting lies in its capacity to give a significant and multifaceted story experience. Dissimilar to customary settings that might zero in exclusively on actual scenes, political interest, or character-driven show, the Congruity

Setting presents a powerful aspect that adds profundity and intricacy to the narrating. It takes into account investigation of existential topics, the interconnectedness, everything being equal, and the fragile equilibrium that supports the texture of the universe.

One of the critical parts of the Concordance Setting is the accentuation on interconnectedness. Elements inside this setting are not detached creatures; all things considered, they are strings woven into the bigger embroidery of the shared perspective. This interconnectedness isn't restricted to people yet stretches out to the actual quintessence of the actual setting. The land, the energy flows, and the substances all add to an amicable entire, making a feeling of solidarity that rises above distinction.

The idea of interconnectedness is intently attached to the center component of Solidarity. As one Setting, Solidarity is definitely not an inactive power however a functioning and dynamic energy that ties everything together.

The ensemble orchestrates the different voices of the universe, making a firm entirety. This accentuation on Solidarity cultivates a feeling of local area and divided predetermination between substances inside the setting, empowering coordinated effort and shared understanding.

Variety, one more center component, adds a layer of extravagance to the Concordance Setting. It isn't simply an acknowledgment of contrasts however a festival of the remarkable characteristics that every substance brings to the vast embroidery. Variety is the flash that lights imagination, presenting a large number of points of view and encounters that add to the general story. The setting turns into a material painted with the lively shades of differed substances, each assuming a fundamental part in the unfurling story.

Harmony, as a center component, guarantees that neither Solidarity nor Variety overpowers the other. The inestimable equilibrium keeps mayhem from destroying the texture of the Concordance Setting. Balance appears in the repeating idea of presence, the back and forth movement of energies that keep everything under control and forestall stagnation. This sensitive equilibrium acquaints a powerful pressure with the setting, where elements should explore the difficulties of keeping up with congruity despite disagreement.

Reverberation, the fourth center component, adds a layer of intricacy to the Congruity Setting. The reverberation of activities and feelings resonates across the embroidery of presence. Reverberation makes associations that rise above reality, connecting substances in manners that go past the prompt. This interconnected snare of thunderous flows adds a feeling of coherence to the story, where the results of past activities wait and shape the present.

Quietness, as the fifth center component, pervades each side of the Congruity Setting with serenity and harmony. It isn't simply a uninvolved state however a functioning power that relieves the injuries of presence. Quietness permits elements to track down comfort and thoughtfulness, encouraging a feeling of equilibrium and prosperity. This center component acquaints a pondering perspective with the setting, empowering characters to consider their activities and look for inward congruity.

Progress, the 6th center component, impels the Congruity Putting forth. The power of progress drives advancement and development. Progress isn't simply mechanical or cultural; it is likewise an individual and otherworldly excursion for substances inside the setting. This center component guarantees that the story isn't stale yet continually advancing, introducing new moves and open doors for characters to investigate and gain from.

Compassion, the seventh and last center component, fills in as the scaffold that associates the unique strings of the Concordance Setting. It is the capacity to comprehend and discuss the thoughts of others, cultivating a profound feeling of association.

Sympathy makes bonds that persevere through difficulties and wins, building up the solidarity of the domain. This center component stresses the significance of connections and close to home associations in molding the account.

The meaning of the Concordance Setting becomes clear in its capacity to give a structure to investigating significant subjects and widespread bits of insight. Through the transaction of the center components, the setting turns into an impression of the intricacies of presence, offering a focal point through what characters and perusers the same can ponder the idea of the real world, the significance of solidarity, and the excellence of variety.

Together as one Setting, narrating takes on a profound and philosophical aspect. The accounts become metaphorical, welcoming perusers to contemplate existential inquiries and dive into the secrets of cognizance. The interconnectedness of substances and the accentuation on center components make a setting where each activity, each decision, and each relationship resounds through the inestimable embroidery, leaving an enduring effect on the story.

The setting's importance is likewise obvious in its ability to move a feeling of marvel and wonder. The vast powers that administer the Agreement Setting are not far off and mysterious; they are essential to the ordinary encounters of substances inside the setting. The scenes are not simply physical; they are appearances of the center components, mirroring the powerful interaction of grandiose powers. This vivid nature of the setting upgrades the peruser's commitment, welcoming them to investigate the complexities of the grandiose dance.

Moreover, the Congruity Setting difficulties customary narrating shows by stressing the recurrent idea of presence. Time in this setting isn't direct yet a persistent circle, reflecting the everlasting dance of the center components. This worldly design presents an extraordinary account musicality, taking into consideration non-direct narrating and a liquid investigation of the past, present, and future. It builds up the immortal idea of the setting, where the reverberations of activities resound across the ages.

The flexibility of reality inside the Concordance Setting adds one more layer of importance. Substances have the capacity to control the center components partially, considering a dynamic and intuitive story experience. This control is definitely not a simple activity of force however an amicable cooperation with the vast powers that shape their reality. Characters can channel the energies of Solidarity, saddle the inventive force of Variety, and tap into the full flows that associate all elements. This intuitive component adds a feeling of organization to the characters and perusers, welcoming them to take part in the unfurling story effectively.

Occupants of the Congruity Setting set out on ventures that rise above the physical and dig into the profound and powerful domains. These excursions are journeys for outside goals as well as significant odysseys of self-revelation and illumination.

Substances look to fall in line with the agreeable progression of the center components, investigating the more profound secrets of presence and advancing because of the grandiose powers that oversee their existence. This accentuation on internal excursions adds a layer of profundity to character improvement and considers a more nuanced investigation of self-improvement and change.

The safe-havens and territories inside the Congruity Setting act as central focuses for reflection, learning, and fellowship. These supernatural areas give characters valuable chances to develop how they might interpret the center components and the grandiose powers that shape their world. The savvy elderly folks and guides inside these territories offer direction to those looking for a more profound association with the supernatural parts of the setting. This mentorship dynamic improves the story by giving characters wellsprings of astuteness and knowledge, further advancing their excursions.

Clashes inside the Concordance Setting are not simple outer fights but rather impressions of unseen conflicts and irregular characteristics in the astronomical dance. In the midst of friction, substances face difficulties that test how they might interpret the center components and their capacity to explore the complex dance of presence. The meaning of contention lies in its groundbreaking potential, offering characters valuable open doors for development, thoughtfulness, and the rebuilding of agreement. Misfortune turns into an impetus for change, and goals are not only outer victories but rather impressions of internal equilibrium and understanding.

The infinite embroidered artwork of the Agreement Setting isn't static however steadily developing. Substances, through their activities and decisions, add to the continuous story of the domain. The setting turns into a no nonsense element formed by the shared mindset of its occupants. The accounts of affection, hardship, win, and misfortune become strings in the excellent embroidery, each adding to the rich and many-sided story of the domain.

2.2 Delve into the interconnectedness of geography, climate, and ecosystems.

Topography, environment, and biological systems structure a mind boggling and interconnected web that shapes the normal world. This reliance is major to the working and supportability of the World's different surroundings. To dive into the complexities of this interconnectedness, one must initially comprehend how geology fills in as the material whereupon different components unfurl.

Geology, the investigation of the World's actual highlights and the circulation of life across its surface, establishes the groundwork for the complicated dance among environment and biological systems.

The geography, landforms, and spatial course of action of topographical elements establish different environments that impact the environment and, thus, the biological systems that flourish inside them. Mountains, valleys, fields, and waterways all add to the territorial and neighborhood varieties in environment that, thusly, shape the biodiversity of biological systems.

Mountains, for instance, assume a significant part in modifying environment designs. As air ascends over mountain ranges, it cools and deliveries dampness, prompting the development of precipitation. This cycle, known as orographic lift, makes unmistakable climatic zones on one or the other side of the mountain. The windward side encounters higher precipitation, cultivating the advancement of lavish environments, while the leeward side, in the downpour shadow, may confront dry circumstances. This geological element, thusly, starts a cascading type of influence that essentially impacts the environment and consequently shapes the biological systems that can flourish in these fluctuated conditions.

Essentially, waterways, like seas and oceans, significantly affect environment and biological systems. Seas go about as intensity sinks, retaining and reallocating sun based energy across the planet. The development of sea flows controls temperature, and the nearness of expanses of land to these flows impacts neighborhood environments. Waterfront regions frequently experience milder temperatures because of the directing impact of adjacent seas. These oceanic environments, portrayed by moderately stable temperatures, make great circumstances for assorted biological systems to thrive.

Topographical elements likewise influence the conveyance of daylight, impacting temperature varieties and establishing unmistakable environment zones. The equator, for example, gets more straightforward daylight consistently, bringing about hotter temperatures. Conversely, the posts get daylight at a slanted point, prompting colder temperatures. These latitudinal varieties in temperature add to the development of environment zones, for example, tropical, subtropical, calm, and polar, each holding onto extraordinary biological systems adjusted to their particular climatic circumstances.

The interconnectedness reaches out to the mind boggling connection among geology and environment. As environment designs are impacted by topographical elements, they, thus, shape the scenes and characterize the sorts of biological systems that can flourish in a specific locale. Desert scenes, described by dry circumstances and negligible precipitation, frequently arise in downpour shadow regions or districts a long way from maritime impacts. These conditions, for example, the Sahara Desert or the Australian Outback, display unmistakable transformations in their environments, highlighting verdure fit for enduring outrageous temperatures and shortage of water.

Alternately, lavish rainforests are many times found in central districts where plentiful daylight and predictable precipitation make ideal circumstances for plant development. The Amazon Rainforest, for example, is complicatedly connected to the geological setting of the Amazon

Bowl, getting abundant measures of precipitation and daylight that support one of the most biodiverse environments on The planet. The geological course of action of landmasses, sea flows, and winning breezes adds to the production of these assorted and concentrated environments, affecting the biological systems they support.

Environment, as a vital middle person in the interconnected set of three, goes about as a scaffold among topography and biological systems. It envelops the drawn out examples of temperature, dampness, wind, and precipitation that characterize a district. The arrangement of environments is frequently founded on the Köppen environment characterization framework, which considers temperature and precipitation to sort districts into particular environment types. Every environment type significantly affects the verdure that can flourish in a given region, showing the personal association among environment and biological systems.

Tropical rainforests, described by high temperatures and steady precipitation consistently, support a mind boggling variety of plant and creature life. The warm and moist circumstances give an ideal climate to the multiplication of species adjusted to the rich biodiversity of these biological systems. Interestingly, polar environments, set apart by low temperatures and restricted precipitation, have strong species like greeneries, lichens, and certain well evolved creatures adjusted to the cruel states of the Cold and Antarctic areas.

The impact of environment on biological systems is additionally exemplified by the advances between environment zones. Ecotones, or momentary zones between various environments, arise where environments meet. For example, the limit between a tropical rainforest and a savannah makes an ecotone known as a tropical occasional timberland. These momentary regions harbor a blend of animal types from the two environments, exhibiting the unique idea of limits molded by climatic circumstances.

The sensitive equilibrium inside environments is kept up with by the perplexing exchange of abiotic and biotic elements, the two of which are significantly affected by environment. Abiotic factors, like temperature, precipitation, and soil structure, straightforwardly influence the sorts of organic entities that can flourish in a given environment. Biotic variables, including connections among species and rivalry for assets, are complicatedly connected to the accessibility of these abiotic factors. Changes in environment, whether progressive or abrupt, can upset this fragile equilibrium, prompting shifts in biological systems and expected dangers to biodiversity.

Environmental change, driven by human exercises and regular cycles, represents a huge test to the interconnected ternion of geology, environment, and biological systems. Changes in temperature, precipitation examples, and ocean levels have sweeping ramifications for the conveyance of species and the working of biological systems.

The climbing worldwide temperatures related with environmental change, for example, may prompt changes in the geological scopes of species as they move to track down appropriate living spaces. The interconnectedness of the group of three implies that adjustments of one part resonate through the others, making flowing consequences for the normal world.

Increasing temperatures can impact the recurrence and power of outrageous climate occasions, like tropical storms, dry seasons, and heatwaves. These occasions, thusly, can significantly affect environments. Backwoods might confront expanded dangers of rapidly spreading fires during delayed dry spells, coral reefs might blanch and debase under raised ocean temperatures, and wetlands might encounter changes in water accessibility. The interconnected idea of topography, environment, and biological systems implies that changes in a single perspective can set off a chain response of natural results.

Ocean level ascent, one more result of environmental change, has direct ramifications for waterfront biological systems and the networks that rely upon them. Low-lying beach front regions might confront expanded flooding and saltwater interruption, influencing the strength of wetlands, mangroves, and estuaries. These environments give basic territories to a great many animal categories, act as nurseries for financially significant fish, and go about as normal cradles against storm floods. The interconnectedness of these beach front biological systems with both geological and climatic variables features the weakness of these conditions to the effects of an evolving environment.

The deficiency of biodiversity, an immediate consequence of environmental change and human exercises, upsets the mind boggling connections inside biological systems. Species that have developed to flourish in unambiguous environments might confront difficulties as their territories change. Thusly, the interconnectedness of environments implies that the downfall or deficiency of one animal groups can have expanding influences all through the whole biological system. For instance, pollinators, for example, honey bees assume an essential part in the multiplication of many plant species. The decay of honey bee populaces because of environmental change and different stressors can have flowing consequences for plant networks, affecting different species that rely upon these plants for food and sanctuary.

Environment benefits, the advantages that people get from biological systems, are likewise personally attached to the interconnected set of three. Environment guideline, water cleansing, and the arrangement of food and assets are biological system benefits that rely upon the wellbeing and working of biological systems. Changes in environment designs, impacted by geological elements, can disturb these administrations, influencing the prosperity of human populaces. For example, adjusted precipitation examples might affect water accessibility, and changes in temperature might influence rural efficiency. The interconnectedness of topography, environment, and environments highlights the significance of protecting and reestablishing these normal frameworks to assist both nature and humankind.

Human exercises, including deforestation, urbanization, and the consuming of petroleum products, add to the disturbance of the interconnected ternion. Deforestation changes scenes, diminishing the degree of backwoods that assume an essential part in controlling environment and supporting biodiversity. Urbanization changes geological highlights, supplanting regular natural surroundings with constructed conditions. The consuming of non-renewable energy sources discharges ozone depleting substances into the environment, adding to a worldwide temperature alteration and changes in environment designs. The outcomes of these human-prompted modifications echo through biological systems, featuring the significant effect of human exercises on the interconnected snare of geology, environment, and environments.

Preservation and economical administration rehearses are fundamental for keeping up with the sensitive equilibrium inside the interconnected ternion. Safeguarded regions, for example, public stops and saves, assume a urgent part in protecting the biodiversity and environmental honesty of biological systems. These regions act as shelters for species, permitting them to flourish in their normal natural surroundings and adding to the general strength of the interconnected web. Supportable land use rehearses, for example, agroforestry and dependable metropolitan preparation, mean to offset human requirements with biological protection, perceiving the significance of safeguarding geological highlights and environment designs for the prosperity of environments.

The mix of environmental change moderation and transformation systems is likewise essential in tending to the difficulties presented by an evolving environment. Relief endeavors center around lessening ozone depleting substance outflows to restrict the degree of environmental change, while variation estimates intend to assist biological systems and human networks with adapting to the inescapable effects. Perceiving the interconnectedness of geology, environment, and biological systems is fundamental for creating all encompassing and successful techniques that think about the more extensive setting of regular frameworks.

Training and mindfulness are incredible assets in cultivating a more profound comprehension of the interconnected set of three and advancing manageable practices. By bringing issues to light about the significance of saving geological highlights, moderating environmental change, and preserving biological systems, people and networks can add to the aggregate work to shield the wellbeing of the planet. Ecological training programs, outreach drives, and support endeavors assume a fundamental part in enabling individuals to settle on informed choices that benefit both the interconnected normal world and human social orders.

Taking everything into account, the interconnectedness of topography, environment, and biological systems shapes the complex woven artwork of the World's regular frameworks. Geology gives the material whereupon environment and biological systems unfurl, molding the scenes and natural surroundings that help a different exhibit of life.

Environment, as the middle person among geology and biological systems, impacts the drawn out examples of temperature, precipitation, and other natural factors that characterize locales. Biological systems, thus, are personally connected to both geology and environment, adjusting to the particular states of their living spaces.

This interconnected group of three is fundamental for the working and manageability of the planet. Changes in a single part resonate through the others, making flowing impacts that influence the wellbeing and strength of regular frameworks. Human exercises, especially those adding to environmental change and natural surroundings annihilation, present critical difficulties to this fragile equilibrium. Preservation, supportable administration practices, and environmental change moderation and transformation are significant for saving the interconnected trap of topography, environment, and biological systems.

Understanding and valuing the significant reliance of these components is critical to encouraging an all encompassing way to deal with natural stewardship. As social orders explore the intricacies of an influencing world, perceiving the interconnectedness of topography, environment, and biological systems is fundamental for making a maintainable and amicable relationship with the normal world.

2.3 Introduce the idea that the setting itself has a character-like role in the narrative.

In the tremendous domain of narrating, the setting is much of the time saw as a background — a phase whereupon characters play out their dramatizations and experiences. Notwithstanding, a more nuanced and enthralling point of view arises when one considers that the actual setting can assume a personality like job in the story. In this story worldview, the setting isn't only a uninvolved scenery yet a functioning member, impacting the story in significant ways and adding to the general climate and subjects of the account.

The idea of the setting as a person is certainly not an original one, yet its importance is frequently disregarded. Past being a simple scenery, the setting has its own character, history, and elements that shape the encounters of the characters and the direction of the story. Similarly as characters go through bends of advancement and change, the setting develops and communicates with the unfurling occasions, turning into a vital piece of the narrating embroidered artwork.

Consider a clamoring city with transcending high rises, neon lights, and swarmed roads. This metropolitan setting, with its dynamic energy and steady development, impacts the speed and tone of the account. The cityscape turns out to be in excess of a detached stage; it turns into a functioning member, forming the encounters of characters who explore its twisted roads. The actual city might have a character — a person with a mind boggling history, temperaments, and a unique presence that impacts the decisions and predeterminations of those inside its limits.

Essentially, a thick and old woods can assume a personality like job. The murmuring leaves, baffling shadows, and the deep rooted trees instill the setting with a feeling of old insight and secret insider facts. The woods turns into a living element, influencing the characters who navigate its profundities. Its personality is uncovered through the difficulties it presents, the animals that stay inside, and the mysterious environment that penetrates the account. The backwoods, basically, turns into a person that shapes the excursion of the people who adventure into its profundities.

In this story worldview, the setting isn't consigned to the foundation however arises as a co-hero — a substance with office and impact. Its personality is characterized by the topographical highlights, environment, authentic occasions, and social components that all in all structure its character. By instilling the setting with these powerful properties, narrators hoist it past a static scenery and permit it to shape the unfurling occasions effectively.

The setting as a person is especially obvious in speculative fiction classifications like dream and sci-fi. In universes where sorcery is genuine, planets are alive, and scenes shift with the impulses of the universe, the setting frequently assumes a critical part in driving the story. Take, for instance, a fantastical domain where the very scene is conscious, answering the feelings and goals of the individuals who possess it. In such a setting, the actual land turns into a person, equipped for helping or preventing the heroes in view of its own inspirations and wants.

Consider a sci-fi story set on a conscious spaceship rushing through the universe. The spaceship isn't only a vessel yet a person with its own cognizance and objectives. Its inner frameworks, man-made brainpower, and the interesting difficulties it presents become fundamental to the story. The spaceship's personality is uncovered through its connections with the team, its reactions to outer dangers, and the advancing connections between the characters and their heavenly habitation.

Indeed, even in additional grounded and reasonable settings, the climate can assume a personality like quality. A little, affectionate town with a rich history and erratic occupants turns out to be something other than an area; it turns into a person with its own eccentricities, customs, and mannerisms. The setting impacts the characters' ways of behaving, shapes the local area elements, and even effects the decisions accessible to the heroes. Along these lines, the town turns into a functioning member in the account, affecting the story's bearing.

The idea of the setting as a person reaches out past the actual scene to incorporate social and verifiable components. A story set against the background of a turbulent political scene, for instance, may highlight the political environment as a person by its own doing. The moving unions, fights for control, and cultural disturbances become dynamic powers that effectively shape the story. In such cases, the setting's personality is characterized by the philosophies, clashes, and cultural standards that portray the world where the story unfurls.

The meaning of the setting as a person lies in its capacity to extend the story and give a more vivid encounter to the crowd. While the setting is treated as a dynamic and developing substance, it adds layers of intricacy to the story. The connections among characters and their current circumstance become more nuanced, and the difficulties they face are not exclusively outside however emerge from the actual idea of the actual setting.

Moreover, the setting as a person adds to the topical wealth of the story. It permits narrators to investigate significant inquiries concerning the connection among people and their environmental factors. Does the setting mirror the characters' conflicts under the surface, or does it go about as a contradiction that challenges their convictions and values? By taking into account the setting as a person, narrators can mesh unpredictable topical strings into the story texture, investigating the cooperative connection among characters and their current circumstance.

To rejuvenate the setting as a person, narrators utilize different scholarly strategies. Distinct language turns into a powerful device for summoning the character of the setting. Rather than simply portraying actual qualities, essayists inject the depictions with emotive language that catches the substance of the climate. By taking advantage of tactile subtleties — sights, sounds, scents, and surfaces — scholars can convey the setting's personality in a manner that resounds with the crowd.

The setting's personality is likewise uncovered through its associations with the heroes. Similarly as characters participate in discourse and struggle, the setting can convey through its difficulties, impediments, and open doors. A cruel desert, for example, may give characters actual preliminaries that reflect their unseen conflicts. A thick and puzzling timberland might disguise privileged insights that challenge the characters to stand up to their feelings of dread. These connections characterize the setting's personality and impact the account's movement.

Besides, the verifiable and social components of the setting add to its personality. The occasions that have formed the world, the practices that characterize its kin, and the aggregate recollections that wait in the air totally become fundamental parts of the setting's personality. Through the investigation of these social and verifiable layers, narrators can reinvigorate the setting, permitting it to resound with legitimacy and profundity.

The climate and environment of a setting assume a significant part in conveying its personality. Similarly as the changing temperaments of a person can impact the tone of a scene, the weather conditions can set the profound background for a story. A blustery night might uplift pressure and hint struggle, while a reasonable, radiant day might summon sensations of peacefulness and trust. By utilizing weather conditions and climatic circumstances purposely, narrators can shape the profound scene of the story and saturate the setting with a particular person.

Consider the imagery that the setting can typify. A forsaken no man's land might represent segregation, despair, and the repercussions of a devastating occasion. A clamoring city might address progress, desire, and the intricacies of present day life. These emblematic components of the setting effectively upgrade its personality, permitting it to convey more profound implications and subjects that resound with the story's center.

The setting as a person likewise offers potential open doors for story development. By obscuring the lines between the physical and supernatural, narrators can make settings that rise above customary limits. In speculative fiction, for instance, universes where the limits between the residing and the non-residing obscure, where scenes answer the feelings of their occupants, or where whole biological systems have awareness can offer new and creative points of view. In these settings, the person like characteristics of the climate are enhanced, making account prospects that go past the limitations of the real world.

The idea of a setting playing a person like job in an account goes past traditional narrating standards, offering a new viewpoint that enhances the profundity and intricacy of a story. In conventional stories, settings are much of the time saw as static sceneries, giving a phase to characters to order their accounts. In any case, while the setting is saturated with dynamic credits, a story arises where the climate effectively shapes the occasions, impacts character curves, and adds to the topical reverberation of the general story.

This story worldview presents the idea that the setting is certainly not an inactive substance however a functioning member with its own character, history, and organization. Similarly as characters go through curves of advancement and change, the setting develops, connects with the unfurling occasions, and turns into a necessary piece of the narrating embroidery. This viewpoint prompts narrators to think about the setting as a co-hero — an element that impacts the story's direction and participates in a harmonious relationship with the characters.

To see the value in the setting as a person, one should dig into the different aspects that add to its personality like job. These aspects incorporate the topographical highlights, environment, verifiable occasions, social components, and, surprisingly, emblematic portrayals that on the whole structure the setting's personality. By investigating these viewpoints, narrators can reinvigorate the setting, permitting it to resound with validness and profundity.

One of the principal components in laying out the setting as a person is the utilization of illustrative language. Instead of introducing the climate as a simple background, essayists utilize emotive language that catches the quintessence of the setting. By taking advantage of tangible subtleties — sights, sounds, scents, and surfaces — journalists can convey the setting's personality in a manner that resounds with the crowd. A clamoring cityscape might be portrayed with lively and vivacious language, while a quiet woods might inspire a feeling of serenity through rich and vivid portrayals.

Moreover, the setting's personality is uncovered through its cooperations with the heroes. Similarly as characters take part in discourse and struggle, the setting imparts through the difficulties, deterrents, and valuable open doors it presents. A brutal desert, for example, may represent difficulty and test the versatility of characters, reflecting their unseen conflicts. On the other hand, a quiet ocean side might offer a scenery for reflection and self-disclosure. These communications effectively characterize the setting's personality and impact the account's movement.

The verifiable and social components of the setting contribute fundamentally to its personality. The occasions that have molded the world, the customs that characterize its kin, and the aggregate recollections that wait in the air become necessary parts of the setting's personality. Through the investigation of these social and verifiable layers, narrators can mix the setting with a rich and nuanced character. A town with a background marked by versatility and local area soul might ooze a person of solidarity and brotherhood, forming the cooperations and connections between its occupants.

The climate and environment of a setting assume a urgent part in conveying its personality. Similarly as characters' mind-sets impact the tone of a scene, the weather conditions can set the close to home background for a story. A turbulent night might elevate pressure and portend struggle, while a reasonable, radiant day might summon sensations of peacefulness and trust. By utilizing weather conditions and climatic circumstances purposely, narrators can shape the profound scene of the story and permeate the setting with a particular person.

Imagery adds one more layer to the setting's personality. The actual scene might turn into a similitude, encapsulating subjects and ideas that reverberate with the overall story. A tough mountain reach might represent difficulties that characters should survive, while an immense and neglected sea might address the obscure and the conceivable outcomes of revelation. By integrating emblematic components, the setting rises above its actual properties, offering a more profound and more full association with the story's subjects.

The idea of the setting as a person turns out to be especially articulated in speculative fiction types like dream and sci-fi. In these classes, settings frequently have fantastical or supernatural characteristics that hoist them past the customary. For instance, an enchanted woods where the trees murmur old insider facts and the very air beats with magical energy turns into a person with organization and impact. The timberland's personality is characterized by its charming environment, its part in the characters' excursions, and own inspirations might line up with or challenge the heroes.

Also, sci-fi stories might include settings that rise above the ordinary comprehension of actual scenes. A space station with computerized reasoning, holographic connection points, and self-supporting environments becomes an area as well as a person with its own cognizance and objectives.

The setting's personality is uncovered through its connections with the team, its reactions to outer dangers, and the developing connections between the characters and their divine homestead.

Indeed, even in additional grounded and practical settings, the climate can assume a personality like quality. An affectionate unassuming community with a rich history, quirky customs, and unconventional occupants turns out to be something other than an area; it turns into a person with its own peculiarities and elements. The setting impacts the characters' ways of behaving, shapes local area associations, and even effects the decisions accessible to the heroes. Along these lines, the town turns into a functioning member in the account, affecting the story's heading.

The meaning of the setting as a person lies in its capacity to develop the story and give a more vivid encounter to the crowd. While the setting is treated as a dynamic and developing substance, it adds layers of intricacy to the story. The cooperations among characters and their current circumstance become more nuanced, and the difficulties they face are not exclusively outside yet emerge from the actual idea of the actual setting.

Besides, the setting as a person adds to the topical extravagance of the story. It permits narrators to investigate significant inquiries regarding the connection among people and their environmental elements. Does the setting mirror the characters' conflicts under the surface, or does it go about as a contradiction that challenges their convictions and values? By taking into account the setting as a person, narrators can mesh unpredictable topical strings into the story texture, investigating the harmonious connection among characters and their current circumstance.

Generally, the setting as a person is a methodology that rises above the conventional limits of narrating, welcoming essayists to see their story scenes with a new and innovative focal point. The setting turns out to be in excess of a background; it turns into a co-maker of the account, molding the occasions, impacting character circular segments, and adding to the topical reverberation of the story. This approach offers potential open doors for account advancement, permitting narrators to investigate dynamic and unpredictable narrating prospects.

To rejuvenate the setting as a person, narrators should utilize different scholarly strategies. Engaging language, as referenced prior, turns into a strong device for inspiring the character of the setting. By injecting depictions with emotive language and taking advantage of tangible subtleties, journalists can make a distinctive and vivid experience for the crowd. Whether it's the hurrying around of a modern city or the serenity of a peaceful glade, the language used to portray the setting shapes its personality.

Discourse and communications among characters and the setting further accentuate its personality like job. Similarly as characters participate in discussions, the setting imparts through its actual characteristics and the difficulties it presents. A run down, deserted building may quietly tell stories of its past, impacting the characters' discernments and choices. Conversely, an energetic commercial center might connect with the characters in a chaos of voices and exercises, forming their encounters and cooperations.

Story viewpoint likewise assumes a vital part in depicting the setting as a person. By taking on a point of view that permits perusers to see the world through the eyes of the setting, scholars can make a more private and vivid association. This viewpoint might include investigating the inward contemplations and inspirations of the setting, uncovering its longings, fears, and developing elements. Whether through a first-individual story according to the point of view of the setting or a third-individual point of view that digs into its inward functions, the account viewpoint adds to the setting's personality.

The pacing of the story likewise impacts how the setting is seen as a person. Similarly as the beat of a story influences the general understanding experience, the pacing can feature various features of the setting's personality. A sluggish and pensive speed might permit perusers to relish the subtleties of a rich and complicated setting, submerging themselves in its subtleties. On the other hand, a high speed story might convey the dynamic and consistently changing nature of the setting, underscoring its job as a functioning member in the unfurling occasions.

The development of the setting all through the story supports its personality like characteristics. Similarly as characters go through circular segments of advancement, the setting might change because of the occasions of the story. This change could be physical, like the changing seasons in a characteristic setting or the structural development of a city over the long run. It could likewise be representative.

Chapter 3

Cultural Foundations

Social establishments structure the bedrock of social orders, giving a rich embroidery that winds around together practices, convictions, and values. These establishments are the strings that associate people to their past, molding their present and affecting their future. Looking at social establishments includes digging into the verifiable, social, and philosophical underpinnings that characterize a local area's personality.

At the core of social establishments lies history — a story that unfurls across ages, conveying the aggregate encounters of a group. History is in excess of a sequential record; a living substance molds social character. Whether it's the old human advancements of Mesopotamia, the administrations of China, or the realms of Rome, each has made a permanent imprint on the social underpinnings of their individual districts.

The social groundworks of a general public are likewise profoundly laced with its social designs. Normal practices, pecking orders, and organizations assume a significant part in forming social personalities. These designs give the structure inside which people explore their lives, affecting everything from familial connections to monetary frameworks. Think about the station framework in India, where social delineation plays generally directed people's parts and open doors in view of birth.

Reasoning goes about as a directing power in social establishments, molding the manner in which individuals see the world and their place in it. From the philosophical insights of old Greek scholars like Socrates and Plato toward the Eastern methods of reasoning of Confucianism and Taoism, these scholarly flows impact cultural qualities, moral standards, and the actual texture of social character.

Religion, as well, is a foundation of social establishments. Whether it's the polytheistic convictions of old civilizations, the monotheistic customs of Judaism, Christianity, and Islam, or the otherworldly acts of native societies, religion gives an ethical compass and a feeling of inspiration. It saturates customs, functions, and day to day existence, interweaving with social practices and molding cultural standards.

Language, as a vehicle of articulation and correspondence, is a powerful power in social establishments. Tongues, phrases, and semantic subtleties convey the quintessence of a culture, mirroring its set of experiences and perspective. The protection of dialects, especially those in danger of eradication, is fundamental for keeping up with the social variety that advances our worldwide embroidery.

Creative articulation, in different structures, is a dynamic sign of social establishments. Visual expressions, writing, music, dance, and theater act as the two mirrors and shapers of society. They embody the aggregate feelings, stories, and yearnings of a group, making social relics that persevere through time. The cavern artworks of Lascaux, the amazing sonnets of Homer, the traditional pieces of Mozart — all add to the social tradition of mankind.

Social establishments are not static; they develop and adjust to evolving conditions. Globalization, mechanical headways, and intercultural collaborations add to the unique idea of social personalities. The mixing of customs, the trading of thoughts, and the rise of half breed societies describe the contemporary scene, testing customary ideas of social immaculateness.

However, in the midst of this dynamism, social establishments give a feeling of progression and personality. They offer a focal point through which people decipher the world and interface with their foundations. In a quickly changing worldwide scene, the safeguarding and festivity of social establishments become pivotal for cultivating figuring out, resilience, and congruity among different networks.

The meaning of social establishments is clear in the customs and functions that imprint key life altering situations. Birth, transitioning, marriage, and demise are in many cases joined by socially unambiguous practices that mirror a local area's qualities and convictions. These transitional experiences act as standards, supporting the connections among people and their social legacy.

Schooling assumes a vital part in communicating social establishments to people in the future. Through formal and casual means, information on language, history, reasoning, and craftsmanship is passed down, guaranteeing the coherence of social character. Schools, families, and networks become conductors for the transmission of values and customs, outfitting people with the devices to explore the intricacies of the advanced world while remaining grounded in their social roots.

Social establishments additionally meet with issues of force and honor. By and large, predominant societies have frequently forced their qualities and standards on underestimated networks, prompting the disintegration of interesting social characters. Expansionism, dominion, and social digestion have left enduring scars on numerous social orders, inciting progressing battles for social conservation and rejuvenation.

The connection between social establishments and character is complicated and multi-layered. People explore a double presence, having a place with a more extensive social system while likewise declaring their exceptional individual personalities. Social character turns into a mosaic, formed by variables like identity, ethnicity, orientation, and individual encounters. The interchange between these components frames a rich embroidery of characters inside a more extensive social setting.

Language, as a vital part of social character, frequently turns into a point of convergence in conversations of legacy conservation. Endeavors to revive imperiled dialects are not just phonetic undertakings; they are demonstrations of social obstruction and strength. Language exemplifies the subtleties of thought, typifies social insight, and fills in as a store of aggregate memory. As dialects disappear, so too does a significant element of social establishments.

In the domain of social establishments, legends and folklore act as vaults of aggregate insight, moral lessons, and social stories. Across societies, fantasies and legends convey significant bits of insight about the human condition, offering experiences into the qualities and convictions that tight spot networks together. Whether it's the Greek legends of divine beings and legends, the Norse adventures of Odin and Thor, or the African folktales that commend the insight of creatures, these accounts persevere as social standards.

Customary expressions and specialties are basic to social establishments, exemplifying the abilities, style, and imagery of a local area. From mind boggling stoneware plans to winding around designs, from native beadwork to the fragile brushstrokes of conventional artworks,

these imaginative articulations convey the quintessence of social character. In a period of large scale manufacturing and globalization, endeavors to save and advance customary craftsmanship become critical for defending social variety.

Food, as well, is a powerful articulation of social establishments. Culinary practices, recipes went down through ages, and the collective demonstration of sharing dinners are basic to social character. The flavors of Indian food, the many-sided kinds of Japanese sushi, the good dishes of Italian pasta — all mirror the special narratives and geologies that shape culinary practices.

Social establishments frequently cross with natural stewardship, as conventional practices and biological information add to manageable living. Native people group, specifically, have long held a profound association with the land, seeing it not simply as an asset but rather as a sacrosanct substance. Customary horticultural practices, protection strategies, and comprehensive ways to deal with nature mirror the reliance of culture and climate.

The effect of globalization on social establishments is a situation with two sides. On one hand, it works with the trading of thoughts, the festival of variety, and the cultivating of culturally diverse comprehension. Then again, it can prompt social homogenization, where predominant worldwide accounts eclipse and minimize nearby practices. The test lies in finding some kind of harmony that considers social trade without dissolving the wealth of different social establishments.

In the computerized age, innovation fills in as both a disruptor and a preserver of social establishments. The web works with the sharing of social articulations on a worldwide scale, empowering people to interface across lines and exhibit their practices. Computerized chronicles and virtual exhibition halls add to the conservation of social relics, making them open to a more extensive crowd. In any case, the computerized domain additionally presents difficulties, as social allocation, falsehood, and the commodification of social images become pervasive issues.

Social establishments assume an essential part in molding the political scenes of countries. Public character frequently draws from a common social legacy, cultivating a feeling of solidarity among different populaces. Be that as it may, the politicization of culture can likewise be a device of prohibition, minimizing minority gatherings and sustaining power lopsided characteristics. The battle for social freedoms and acknowledgment is entwined with more extensive developments for civil rights and fairness.

In tending to the difficulties confronting social establishments, the idea of social tact arises as an incredible asset. Social discretion perceives the job of culture in cultivating global comprehension and joint effort.

Through social trade programs, creative joint efforts, and instructive drives, countries can fabricate spans, separate generalizations, and advance shared regard. Social strategy goes past political way of talking, encouraging individuals to-individuals associations that rise above international limits.

3.1 Explore how culture shapes the world and vice versa.

Culture isn't just a scenery to human life; a powerful power shapes the world and, thus, is formed by it. This corresponding connection among culture and the world is intricate, complex, and significant, affecting everything from individual convictions to cultural designs and worldwide collaborations. To investigate how culture shapes the world as well as the other way around is to dive into the mind boggling interaction of thoughts, practices, and values that characterize human life.

At its center, culture incorporates the common convictions, values, customs, and ways of behaving that portray a gathering. It is a focal point through which people decipher the world, figure out their encounters, and explore their connections. Whether communicated through language, craftsmanship, religion, or normal practices, culture gives a structure to grasping the human condition.

Language, as an essential vehicle of social articulation, shapes the manner in which people see and speak with the world. Every language conveys its own subtleties, sayings, and social undertones, affecting how individuals put themselves out there as well as how they conceptualize reality. The Sapir-Whorf speculation sets that language influences thought, proposing that the construction and jargon of a language straightforwardly influence mental cycles. As people convey inside the system of their etymological and social setting, they add to the continuous forming of social stories.

Imaginative articulation, one more feature of culture, is a strong power that reflects and shapes cultural qualities. Visual expressions, writing, music, dance, and theater act as mirrors that encapsulate an overall setting. Imaginative manifestations convey tasteful inclinations as well as the hidden social, political, and philosophical flows of a culture. Think about the Renaissance in Europe, where craftsmanship turned into a vehicle for humanism and a festival of independence, impacting the course of Western social turn of events.

Religion, profoundly entwined with culture, assumes a huge part in forming perspectives and moral structures. Conviction frameworks impact individual way of behaving and cultural standards, giving a feeling of motivation, profound quality, and local area. The effect of strict convictions on culture is obvious in customs, services, and moral codes that guide people's lives. Alternately, culture likewise shapes strict articulation, as understandings of strict texts and practices shift across various social settings.

Social designs, including relational intricacies, orientation jobs, and cultural orders, are fundamental parts of culture that impact individual way of behaving and shape aggregate personalities. The jobs relegated to people inside a general public, in view of variables like orientation, age, and social class, are results of social standards and assumptions. The developing idea of these designs reflects progressing cultural changes and difficulties to customary standards, as found in developments pushing for orientation uniformity and civil rights.

Social qualities impact monetary frameworks, deciding examples of creation, utilization, and exchange. The Protestant hard working attitude, for instance, has been credited with molding the advancement of free enterprise in Western social orders, underlining difficult work, frugality, and individual obligation. Likewise, societies that focus on shared prosperity over individual addition might encourage monetary frameworks in light of standards of aggregate possession and rearrangement. The crossing point of culture and financial aspects features the equal connection between cultural qualities and material circumstances.

Globalization, with its interconnected organizations of correspondence, exchange, and social trade, has increased the interchange among culture and the world. While globalization works with the dispersal of social thoughts on a worldwide scale, it likewise raises worries about social homogenization and the disintegration of neighborhood customs. The spread of Western mainstream society, frequently worked with by broad communications and innovation, has provoked banters about social colonialism and the conservation of assorted social characters.

In the domain of legislative issues, culture shapes the arrangement of public personalities and impacts international elements. Patriotism, established from a common perspective of culture, history, and personality, assumes an essential part in molding worldwide relations. Clashes frequently emerge from social contrasts, as countries affirm their extraordinary characters and strive for acknowledgment on the worldwide stage. Conciliatory collaborations, deals, and collusions are formed by social contemplations, mirroring the impact of social qualities on the quest for political targets.

Social tact arises as an essential device in exploring worldwide relations, cultivating common comprehension, and building spans across different societies. Through social trade programs, cooperative creative drives, and instructive organizations, countries try to advance a positive picture, scatter generalizations, and lay out associations at the social level. Social discretion perceives that common social encounters can rise above political contrasts, adding to an additional serene and interconnected world.

The ecological effect of human social orders is likewise formed by social qualities and practices. Native societies, for instance, frequently show a profound association with the regular world, seeing the climate not only as an asset but rather as a consecrated element.

Conventional biological information, went down through ages, reflects maintainable practices that focus on the protection of environments. Conversely, societies driven by industrialism and transient increases might add to ecological corruption.

Mechanical headways, while driven by logical developments, are additionally profoundly impacted by social qualities and needs. The turn of events and reception of advancements reflect cultural requirements, values, and moral contemplations. The plan of innovation, from UIs to calculations, is much of the time molded by social suppositions and predispositions, impacting the manner in which people collaborate with and see mechanical progressions. As innovation turns into an inexorably vital piece of day to day existence, the proportional connection among culture and innovation turns out to be more articulated.

Social mentalities toward training and information procurement add to examples of scholarly advancement inside social orders. The accentuation on scholastic accomplishment, decisive reasoning, and the quest for information changes across societies, molding school systems and the potential open doors accessible to people. Social qualities with respect to schooling impact the improvement of abilities, the transmission of social information, and the development of cultural mentalities toward scholarly pursuits.

Relocation and social trade, whether driven by monetary variables, struggle, or individual decision, add to the dissemination of social components across geological limits. Diaspora people group assume a urgent part in keeping up with and developing social practices outside their nations of beginning. As people and networks explore the intricacies of multiculturalism, the mixing and hybridization of societies bring about new articulations and characters, testing customary thoughts of social virtue.

The job of culture in forming view of wellbeing and prosperity is clear in clinical works on, recuperating customs, and ways to deal with emotional well-being. Social convictions impact's comprehension people might interpret ailment, the utilization of conventional cures, and mentalities toward present day medical care frameworks. The mix of social capability in medical services rehearses perceives the significance of understanding assorted social points of view to give compelling and deferential consideration.

The proportional connection among culture and character is a principal part of human life. Individual characters are formed by social affiliations, enveloping perspectives like identity, ethnicity, religion, and language. Simultaneously, people add to the continuous forming of social characters through their convictions, ways of behaving, and inventive articulations. The exchange among individual and social character is a powerful interaction that happens inside the more extensive setting of cultural standards and values.

In analyzing how culture shapes the world as well as the other way around, perceiving the power elements intrinsic in social interactions is fundamental. Prevailing societies frequently apply impact over minimized or inferior societies, prompting the assignment or deletion of novel social articulations. The battles for social safeguarding and rejuvenation, especially among native networks, feature the continuous difficulties of saving social variety even with globalization and social authority.

3.2 Discuss the influence of history, traditions, and belief systems on the setting.

The setting of any general public is unpredictably woven with the strings of its set of experiences, customs, and conviction frameworks. These components act as the establishment whereupon the physical, social, and social scenes of a spot are developed. Grasping the impact of history, customs, and conviction frameworks on the setting permits us to disentangle the intricacies of human social orders, investigating what the previous shapes the present and means for what's to come.

History, as a living embroidery of occasions and stories, creates a long shaded area over the setting of any general public. The verifiable setting of a spot shapes its actual climate, cultural designs, and social personality. Think about the old city of Rome, where the remains of the Colosseum and the Discussion stand as substantial leftovers of a strong domain. The verifiable layers of victories, relocations, and unrests leave engraves on scenes, impacting engineering, city arranging, and the general person of a setting.

Frontier chronicles, set apart by the development of domains and the inconvenience of unfamiliar rule, significantly affect the settings of numerous locales. The hints of imperialism are apparent in the design of frontier time structures, the burden of Western general sets of laws, and the persevering through traditions of social digestion. The setting turns into a palimpsest, taking the stand concerning the complicated transaction of force elements, opposition, and social hybridization.

Customs, went down through ages, add to the forming of a general public's setting. These customs manifest in ceremonies, services, and ordinary practices that characterize the social scene. In Japan, for example, the setting is profoundly affected by conventional tea functions, cherry bloom celebrations, and the complex plan of Japanese nurseries. These customs decorate the actual climate as well as mirror a significant association with nature, otherworldliness, and a feeling of concordance.

Social customs additionally track down articulation in the plan of residences, metropolitan spaces, and public design. Customary lodging styles, for example, the patio places of China or the adobe designs of native networks, reflect useful contemplations as well as social qualities and social designs.

Conventional commercial centers, sanctuaries, and public social event spaces become hubs of social articulation inside the setting, encouraging a feeling of local area and progression.

Conviction frameworks, whether strict or philosophical, apply a critical effect on the setting of a general public. The glory of Gothic churches in Europe, the multifaceted plans of Hindu sanctuaries in India, and the straightforwardness of Buddhist cloisters in Tibet — all bear the permanent characteristic of strict convictions. These hallowed spaces act as spots of love as well as shape the feel, engineering, and social elements of their environmental factors.

Strict convictions frequently impact the design of urban communities and the association of room. The plan of journey courses, the direction of holy locales, and the development of strict landmarks add to the general setting. In urban communities like Jerusalem, where different strict practices join, the setting turns into a mosaic of hallowed spaces, mirroring the conjunction and clashes intrinsic in assorted conviction frameworks.

Past coordinated religions, conviction frameworks additionally incorporate philosophical and social points of view that shape cultural qualities. Confucianism, with its accentuation on various leveled connections and obedient devotion, has affected the setting in East Asian social orders, affecting family structures, school systems, and normal practices. Additionally, the Illumination beliefs of individual freedom and reason have made a permanent imprint on the settings of Western social orders, affecting political designs, overall sets of laws, and the idea of public spaces.

The impact of history, customs, and conviction frameworks on the setting stretches out to the domain of social scenes. Social scenes, perceived by UNESCO as articulations of human inventiveness and congruity, are molded by the connection among individuals and their current circumstance after some time. The terraced rice fields of Bali, the noteworthy focus of Florence, and the social scene of the Nile Valley — all give testimony regarding the manners by which human social orders have changed and adjusted their surroundings.

Urbanization, driven by verifiable and financial elements, significantly affects the setting of urban communities. The modern transformation, for instance, prompted the fast extension of urban communities, the advancement of production line areas, and the rise of new friendly classes. The setting of modern urban areas, described by manufacturing plants, apartments, and swarmed metropolitan spaces, mirrors the financial changes achieved by industrialization.

The setting of rustic scenes, as well, is molded by authentic practices, for example, agribusiness, land use, and asset the executives. Conventional cultivating techniques, impacted by environment, geography, and social practices, add to the unmistakable examples of provincial settings. The social meaning of specific yields, the plan of farming patios, and the utilization of public spaces for ceremonies and festivities are undeniably implanted in the setting of country scenes.

Struggle and war, critical parts in the authentic story of social orders, leave persevering through engraves on the setting. The scars of combat zones, war remembrances, and remade urban communities recount accounts of versatility, misfortune, and remaking. Post-struggle settings frequently wrestle with the test of revamping actual framework while tending to the injury and social disengagement brought about by war.

The setting turns into a material for memorialization, with landmarks and exhibition halls filling in as tokens of verifiable occasions. The Hiroshima Harmony Dedication in Japan, the Holocaust commemorations in Europe, and the Vietnam Veterans Remembrance in the US — all stand as demonstrations of the getting through effect of authentic injuries on the settings of various social orders.

With regards to native networks, the setting is profoundly associated with tribal terrains and customary practices. Native information frameworks, molded by hundreds of years of communication with the climate, add to maintainable land use, asset the board, and the safeguarding of biodiversity. The settings of native domains frequently mirror an agreeable connection among individuals and nature, testing predominant stories of double-dealing and ecological corruption.

The social setting of a general public isn't static; it develops and adjusts to evolving conditions. Globalization, mechanical progressions, and social trade add to the unique idea of social settings. The spread of worldwide mainstream society, worked with by broad communications and the web, impacts the feel, ways of life, and utilization designs inside assorted settings. The worldwide dissemination of thoughts, pictures, and items makes a social interconnectedness that rises above geological limits.

Social globalization, nonetheless, likewise raises worries about the homogenization of settings and the deficiency of social variety. The strength of Western social standards in the worldwide field has provoked banters about social government and the conservation of nearby customs. Endeavors to shield social legacy, whether through UNESCO assignments or neighborhood drives, become pivotal for keeping up with the genuineness and variety of social settings.

The travel industry, as a type of social trade, adversely affects the settings of social orders. While the travel industry can add to monetary turn of events and multifaceted comprehension, it likewise acts difficulties such like over-the travel industry, social allotment, and the commodification of neighborhood customs. Adjusting the monetary advantages of the travel industry with the protection of social honesty requires smart preparation, manageable practices, and local area commitment.

All in all, the impact of history, customs, and conviction frameworks on the setting is a perplexing and complex exchange that shapes the physical, social, and social scenes of social orders. The engraving of verifiable occasions, the progression of customs, and the core values of conviction frameworks leave enduring engravings on the spots we occupy. Understanding these impacts permits us to see the value in the lavishness of social variety, the strength of human social orders, and the manners by which the past reverberations in the present. The setting, as an impression of aggregate memory and personality, turns into a material whereupon the narratives of human social orders unfurl.

3.3 Address the role of diverse cultures and their interactions in creating a harmonious world.

The job of different societies and their cooperations in making an amicable world is a significant and complicated part of human life. Societies, with their interesting practices, dialects, conviction frameworks, and customs, add to the rich embroidered artwork of humankind. As social orders become progressively interconnected through globalization, innovation, and worldwide relations, the meaning of understanding and valuing different societies becomes central in cultivating a world described by common regard, collaboration, and concordance.

Social variety is a crucial part of the human experience, mirroring the bunch manners by which people and networks explore the world. It envelops not just the apparent parts of culture, like language, dress, and food, yet additionally the immaterial components like qualities, perspectives, and accepted practices. Embracing social variety includes perceiving and commending the distinctions that make each culture remarkable while settling on something worth agreeing on that advances solidarity and understanding.

Language, as a critical part of social character, assumes a pivotal part in molding how people see and communicate with the world. Multilingualism is a demonstration of the variety of human articulation, with large number of dialects spoken across the globe. Language fills in as a vault of social information, sending customs, stories, and perspectives from one age to another. Saving etymological variety isn't just fundamental for keeping up with social character yet additionally for encouraging viable correspondence and diverse comprehension.

Associations between different societies happen on different levels — locally, broadly, and around the world. At the nearby level, networks with a blend of social foundations make energetic and dynamic social spaces. Metropolitan focuses, specifically, frequently act as mixtures where individuals from various societies coincide, carrying with them an abundance of viewpoints, customs, and encounters. In such settings, social connections add to a mosaic of impacts that shape the personality of neighborhoods, organizations, and social elements.

Public social associations are obvious in the different creation of present day country states. Movement, authentic relocations, and diaspora networks add to the social texture of nations. Countries become storehouses of a large number of customs, dialects, and conviction frameworks, mirroring the interconnected narratives of different networks. Public personality, molded by the interaction of societies, fills in as a binding together power that rises above individual contrasts and encourages a feeling of having a place.

Worldwide social communications, energized by propels in innovation and expanded versatility, have advanced in the contemporary world. The progression of data, thoughts, and individuals across borders has prompted a worldwide trade of societies. Mainstream society, impacted by music, film, design, and computerized media, turns into a worldwide peculiarity that rises above topographical limits. While this interconnectedness brings open doors for social improvement, it additionally raises difficulties connected with social homogenization, appointment, and the protection of neighborhood customs.

Chasing an amicable world, the acknowledgment of social privileges and the advancement of social variety are fundamental standards. UNESCO, through drives like the Show on the Security and Advancement of the Variety of Social Articulations, underscores the significance of shielding social variety for the purpose of guaranteeing the prospering of societies around the world. The right to social personality, as expressed in global basic freedoms structures, highlights the benefit of protecting and advancing different societies.

Strict variety, a critical part of social pluralism, assumes a focal part in molding the collaborations between various networks. The world is home to a huge number of strict customs, each with its own convictions, practices, and ceremonies. Interfaith discourse turns into a vital device in cultivating understanding and resistance among different strict networks. Perceiving the common qualities and moral rules that underlie different confidence customs adds to building spans and advancing serene concurrence.

Schooling arises as a critical instrument in advancing social comprehension and encouraging a worldwide viewpoint. Educational programs that consolidate assorted social points of view, chronicles, and commitments assist with developing liberality and compassion among understudies. Openness to various societies through trade programs, language learning, and multicultural drives empowers people to see the value in the wealth of human variety. Instructive establishments, as social center points, assume a significant part in molding people in the future with the abilities and mentalities important for exploring a globalized world.

Social strategy, as a type of worldwide relations, looks to construct spans between countries through the trading of social articulations. Social trade programs, creative coordinated efforts, and drives that feature the variety of world societies add to encouraging common regard and understanding.

The force of social discretion lies in its capacity to rise above political contrasts and make associations at the human level, advancing a common feeling of worldwide citizenship.

Artistic expression, as articulations of social personality, act as all inclusive dialects that can connect social partitions. Writing, visual expressions, music, dance, and theater convey the human involvement with ways that resound across social limits. Craftsmen, as social representatives, can impart shared feelings, values, and yearnings, cultivating associations that rise above etymological and social contrasts. Worldwide coordinated efforts in artistic expressions add to a worldwide social discourse that praises the lavishness of human imagination.

Social celebrations, festivities, and occasions become stages for displaying the variety of world societies. Global celebrations that feature music, cooking, dance, and customs give potential chances to individuals from various foundations to meet up out of a feeling of festivity. These get-togethers cultivate a feeling of shared mankind and make spaces for exchange that rise above public boundaries. Social celebrations add to separating generalizations, dissipating biases, and encouraging a feeling of solidarity in variety.

The job of media in molding discernments and impacting social associations couldn't possibly be more significant. Broad communications, including TV, film, and computerized stages, has the ability to shape accounts, impact popular assessment, and either support or challenge social generalizations. Mindful media rehearses that focus on variety, portrayal, and the advancement of exact social depictions add to building an additional comprehensive and amicable world. Media education, as a fundamental expertise, enables people to draw in with different social portrayals and stories basically.

The work environment, as a microcosm of society, assumes a critical part in molding social collaborations. Variety and consideration drives inside associations add to establishing conditions where people from various social foundations feel esteemed and regarded. Multifaceted correspondence preparing, coaching in racial awareness, and comprehensive recruiting rehearses upgrade social ability among representatives. A different and comprehensive working environment reflects cultural qualities as well as encourages imagination, development, and a feeling of having a place among representatives.

In the domain of worldwide collaboration and strategy, the significance of perceiving and regarding assorted societies couldn't possibly be more significant. Worldwide difficulties, for example, environmental change, general wellbeing emergencies, and monetary imbalances, require cooperative endeavors that rise above public limits. In such settings, social comprehension turns into a urgent consider building trust and working with compelling correspondence among countries. Conciliatory endeavors that consider social subtleties add to the progress of global drives and arrangements.

The conservation of native societies, frequently confronting the danger of termination, is a basic part of cultivating worldwide social concordance. Native people group, with their remarkable dialects, customs, and biological information, add to the variety of human societies. Perceiving and regarding the freedoms of native people groups to their familial grounds, self-assurance, and social practices is a stage toward redressing verifiable treacheries and guaranteeing the endurance of social variety.

Difficulties to making an amicable world through social connections incorporate issues of social assignment, generalizing, and inconsistent power elements. Social appointment, when components of one culture are embraced by individuals from one more culture without appropriate comprehension or regard, can prompt the eradication of social implications and add to social commodification. Aversion to control uneven characters and the enhancement of minimized voices are fundamental in encouraging moral and impartial social collaborations.

collaborations, and effectively advancing the standards of resilience, understanding, and regard. This comprehensive methodology stretches out to different components of human life, including social, financial, political, and instructive domains. As we dig into the complicated elements of social collaborations, we uncover the capability of different societies to add to the making of an amicable world.

One basic part of encouraging social amicability lies in recognizing and valuing the characteristic worth of each culture. Each culture typifies an exceptional arrangement of customs, convictions, practices, and lifestyles that add to the aggregate human experience. Perceiving the extravagance and variety of these social articulations is fundamental in developing an air of shared regard. Instead of survey variety as a wellspring of division, social orders can embrace it as a wellspring of solidarity, learning, and improvement.

Training arises as a vital device in molding perspectives and advancing social comprehension. Schooling systems that coordinate different viewpoints into educational programs, open understudies to different societies, and empower decisive contemplating social issues assume a critical part as one. Past the transmission of information, instruction fills in for of dispersing generalizations, testing predispositions, and sustaining receptiveness. Comprehensive instructive practices add to the advancement of worldwide residents who appreciate and regard the variety of societies.

Language, as a transporter of culture, assumes a focal part in social cooperations. Multilingualism and language variety are resources that add to powerful correspondence and diverse comprehension. Language capability works with relational associations as well as permits people to get to the abundance of social information implanted in semantic articulations. Endeavors to safeguard and elevate semantic variety add to the more extensive objective of keeping up with social extravagance.

Social connections are significantly affected by media and correspondence stages. Broad communications, including TV, film, writing, and advanced media, shape insights, send social stories, and impact general assessment. Dependable media rehearses that focus on exact social portrayals, keep away from generalizations, and elevate variety add to a more comprehensive and agreeable worldwide talk. Media education, as a fundamental ability, enables people to basically draw in with social accounts and challenge one-sided depictions.

Workmanship and social articulations act as extensions that interface individuals across different foundations. Human expression, enveloping visual expressions, music, dance, writing, and theater, offer an all inclusive language that rises above etymological and social limits. Social trades in the domain of expressions add to the production of shared social encounters, cultivating associations that go past international partitions. Worldwide joint efforts in artistic expressions work with the trading of thoughts, viewpoints, and imaginative articulations, cultivating a feeling of interconnectedness.

Social celebrations and occasions assume a crucial part in uniting individuals, praising variety, and cultivating understanding. Celebrations that exhibit music, dance, cooking, and customs give open doors to people to drench themselves in various societies. These social festivals make spaces for discourse, appreciation, and the producing of associations. Partaking in or going to far-reaching developments permits people to encounter the energy and uniqueness of different societies firsthand, encouraging a feeling of shared humankind.

With regards to working environment conditions, advancing social variety and incorporation is vital to making agreeable connections. Associations that focus on variety and carry out comprehensive practices benefit from a large number of viewpoints, encounters, and gifts. Variety in the work environment adds to imagination, development, and a positive hierarchical culture. Endeavors to advance social skill, give racial awareness schooling, and lay out comprehensive strategies add to building an amicable workplace where people feel esteemed and regarded.

Global participation and tact are fundamental fields where the job of different societies in making an amicable world becomes clear. Strategic endeavors that perceive and regard social contrasts add to building trust and understanding among countries. Social tact, including the trading of social articulations, instructive drives, and creative joint efforts, upgrades individuals to-individuals associations and cultivates positive worldwide relations. Recognizing the social subtleties that shape discretionary cooperations is pivotal in building spans and conquering expected social mistaken assumptions.

Strict variety, a huge element of social pluralism, requires nuanced ways to deal with cultivate agreeable collaborations. Interfaith discourse, described by conscious discussions among people of various strict practices, adds to common getting it and participation.

Perceiving the common moral standards and values that underlie different confidence customs makes shared conviction for cooperation on friendly, natural, and helpful issues. Strict resilience and regard for different conviction frameworks are fundamental in making a reality where people can exist together agreeably.

Ecological maintainability is another basic viewpoint where social collaborations assume a huge part. Native societies, specifically, frequently have customary environmental information that adds to maintainable land use and asset the executives. Perceiving and regarding native privileges to their hereditary grounds, integrating customary practices into ecological protection endeavors, and encouraging a comprehensive comprehension of the interconnectedness of people and nature add to worldwide maintainability.

Compromise and peacebuilding endeavors benefit from a comprehension of social elements and authentic settings. Social responsiveness in tending to clashes includes perceiving the effect of verifiable injuries, recognizing different viewpoints, and integrating social customs into compromise processes. In post-struggle settings, social legacy conservation and rejuvenation become essential to revamping networks and encouraging a feeling of personality and coherence.

Worldwide financial communications offer the two potential open doors and difficulties with regards to social variety. Monetary globalization has prompted expanded exchange, venture, and versatility of labor and products across borders. While monetary collaborations add to social trades and the dispersal of items from various societies, they likewise present difficulties connected with social commodification and the expected abuse of social components. Moral contemplations in monetary practices incorporate fair exchange, social property privileges, and the assurance of native information.

Common liberties, as an all inclusive system, highlight the significance of safeguarding and advancing social variety. Social freedoms, including the option to take part in social life, the right to schooling in one's own way of life, and the option to safeguard and foster one's social personality, are basic to cultivating an amicable world. Regarding social privileges includes perceiving the organization of people and networks in deciding their social practices and articulations.

The job of state run administrations in advancing social variety and agreeable associations is critical. Approaches that help social safeguarding, safeguard minority freedoms, and elevate comprehensive practices add to building socially strong social orders. Regulation that tends to separation, bigotry, and social allocation establishes conditions where people can completely partake in open existence unafraid of underestimation. Government drives that help social trade programs, worldwide coordinated efforts, and social tact further improve worldwide comprehension and collaboration.

One test in advancing amicable social collaborations lies in resolving issues of social apportionment and power irregular characteristics. Social allocation happens when components of one culture are embraced by individuals from one more culture without legitimate comprehension or regard. This can prompt the commodification of social images, eradication of social implications, and the propagation of unsafe generalizations. Perceiving and redressing power awkward nature is fundamental in establishing conditions where social communications depend on uniformity, common regard, and shared benefits.

Chapter 4

Flora and Fauna

Greenery, the energetic embroidery of life that decorates our planet, are complicatedly woven into the texture of Earth's biological systems. These different types of life, going from the littlest microorganisms to the transcending trees, make an agreeable equilibrium that supports the fragile trap of life. The expression "greenery" alludes to the vegetation, while "fauna" incorporates the collective of animals. Together, they shape the climate in which they exist, each assuming an essential part in keeping up with environmental harmony.

In the domain of vegetation, the plant realm unfurls an entrancing exhibit of varieties, shapes, and sizes. From the tiny green growth that dance in sunlit waters to the giant sequoias that stand as transcending sentinels in antiquated timberlands, plants encapsulate the quintessence of life on The planet. Photosynthesis, the extraordinary cycle by which plants convert daylight into energy, is a key instrument that supports their own reality as well as fills in as the essential wellspring of sustenance for the whole pecking order.

Inside the complex universe of plants, biodiversity becomes the dominant focal point. Rainforests, with their rich shelters and overflowing undergrowth, exhibit a stunning variety of vegetation. Orchids hang carefully from branches, their unpredictable blossoms welcoming pollinators into an entrancing dance of life. Conversely, parched deserts harbor strong succulents and prickly plants, adjusted to flourish in unforgiving, water-scant conditions. Fields influence with the musicality of the breeze, facilitating a heap of grass animal groups that give food to herbivores.

Blooming plants, with their enrapturing blooms, have advanced perplexing conceptive systems. Honey bees, butterflies, and different pollinators assume a urgent part in this dance of spread, moving dust starting with one bloom then onto the next. This cooperative relationship guarantees the continuation of plant species and features the interconnectedness of life in the normal world.

The fauna, then again, presents a dynamic and different cluster of creatures, each adjusted to their particular biological specialty. From the minute tiny fish that float in the seas to the magnificent elephants that meander the savannas, the animals of the world collectively shows an unmatched range of shapes, sizes, and ways of behaving.

In the profundities of the seas, where daylight battles to enter, odd and entrancing animals call the pit home. Bioluminescent organic entities light up the obscurity, making a powerful scene that remains to a great extent stowed away from natural eyes. Coral reefs, energetic biological systems of marine life, have a submerged fair of varieties as fish dart among the coral arrangements.

Earthbound scenes, as well, are energized by the presence of fauna. In thick wildernesses, the cadenced calls of primates resonate through the trees, while extraordinary birds parade their plumage in a stunning presentation. In polar areas, where the virus chomps perseveringly, strong animals like polar bears and penguins have adjusted to get by in outrageous circumstances. The immeasurability of the animals of the world collectively mirrors the flexibility and versatility of life despite different natural difficulties.

Relocation, a peculiarity implanted in the way of behaving of numerous species, adds a captivating aspect to the universe of fauna. Birds cross landmasses looking for ideal favorable places, whales set out on amazing excursions across seas, and butterflies shudder across scenes in complicated designs. These movements not just feature the natural impulses of these animals yet in addition underline the interconnectedness of environments on a worldwide scale.

As biological systems advance and face difficulties, the fragile harmony among greenery turns out to be progressively helpless to disturbances. Human exercises, going from deforestation to environmental change, significantly affect the complex connections that administer the normal world.

Deforestation, driven by the interest for lumber and rural extension, brings about the deficiency of urgent environments for endless species. The results echo through biological systems, prompting the decay of both plant and creature populaces.

Environmental change, energized by human exercises like the consuming of petroleum derivatives, has expansive impacts on the dispersion and conduct of vegetation. Increasing temperatures, adjusted precipitation examples, and outrageous climate occasions present remarkable difficulties to the versatility of numerous species. Coral reefs, delicate to changes in temperature, face fading occasions that undermine the lively networks they support. Polar bears, reliant upon ocean ice for hunting, wrestle with contracting ice cover in their living spaces.

The deficiency of biodiversity, driven by human exercises, is a worldwide worry with significant ramifications for the strength of the planet. The elimination of species upsets the mind boggling equilibrium of biological systems, possibly prompting flowing impacts that resound across the established pecking order. Preservation endeavors, hence, assume an essential part in relieving the effects of human exercises on greenery.

Safeguarded regions, for example, public parks and untamed life holds, act as safe-havens for a different cluster of animal categories. These spaces give a shelter to plants and creatures to flourish without the prompt dangers presented by human infringement. Protection drives, both at neighborhood and worldwide scales, plan to save and reestablish territories, battle unlawful untamed life exchange, and bring issues to light about the significance of biodiversity.

Notwithstanding the immediate dangers presented by human exercises, backhanded outcomes, for example, the presentation of intrusive species further confound the difficulties looked by local vegetation. Intrusive species, frequently presented unexpectedly by people, can outcompete local species for assets and upset laid out biological connections. This peculiarity has been seen on islands, where presented hunters have crushed populaces of endemic birds and other natural life.

The perplexing exchange among vegetation reaches out past the domain of individual species to include whole environments. Wetlands, for instance, act as essential natural surroundings for a bunch of plant and creature species. The complicated trap of life in wetlands incorporates creatures of land and water, birds, and a different cluster of vegetation. Past giving a home to various animal groups, wetlands offer fundamental environment administrations, for example, water filtration and flood control.

The complex dance among widely varied vegetation isn't restricted to normal environments alone; it additionally stretches out to farming scenes formed by human exercises. Conventional farming practices, well established in the information on neighborhood networks, have supported the conjunction of yields and trained animals for quite a long time.

Be that as it may, current modern horticulture, portrayed by monoculture and escalated asset use, affects biodiversity.

The utilization of pesticides and manures in modern agribusiness influences the designated nuisances and plants as well as has potentially negative side-effects for non-target species. Pollinators, fundamental for the proliferation of many blooming plants, face dangers from pesticide openness, prompting decreases in honey bee populaces. The deficiency of pollinators has flowing consequences for biological systems, influencing the proliferation of plants and the creatures that rely upon them for food.

Hereditary adjustment of harvests, one more sign of present day farming, acquaints novel difficulties with the fragile equilibrium of biological systems. The accidental spread of hereditarily altered creatures (GMOs) raises worries about their expected effect on non-GMO yields and wild family members. The drawn out environmental impacts of inescapable GMO development stay a subject of continuous examination and discussion.

As mankind wrestles with the outcomes of its effect on the regular world, there is a developing acknowledgment of the requirement for reasonable practices that cultivate the concurrence of human exercises and biodiversity. Reasonable turn of events, an idea that tries to address the issues of the present without compromising the capacity of people in the future to address their own issues, lies at the core of endeavors to accommodate the connection among mankind and the normal world.

Preservation science, an interdisciplinary field that draws on biology, hereditary qualities, and other logical disciplines, assumes a crucial part in understanding and tending to the difficulties looked by greenery. Preservation researcher work to unwind the intricacies of environments, recognize key species for preservation, and foster methodologies to safeguard and reestablish natural surroundings. Cooperative endeavors between researchers, policymakers, and nearby networks are fundamental to executing viable preservation measures.

Even with worldwide difficulties, for example, environmental change and natural surroundings misfortune, preservation drives progressively perceive the significance of safeguarding and reestablishing biological systems at a scene scale. Availability between safeguarded regions and the rebuilding of hallways that work with the development of species can upgrade the versatility of biodiversity despite natural changes. Huge scope protection endeavors, for example, the renewed introduction of cornerstone species and the production of natural life passageways, plan to address the more extensive biological setting in which verdure associate.

Past the domain of science and strategy, social and native viewpoints offer important bits of knowledge into the mind boggling connections among people and the normal world. Native information, went down through ages, frequently holds significant insight about maintainable practices and the conjunction of networks with their current circumstance.

Perceiving and regarding native viewpoints is basic to manufacturing a way toward a more amicable connection among mankind and the planet.

4.1 Examine the impact of unique plant and animal life on the setting.

The effect of novel plant and creature life on the setting is a complex and vital part of the regular world. Biological systems, formed by the interchange of widely varied vegetation, are dynamic and strong conditions that add to the general soundness of the planet. This complex relationship reaches out from the minute level, where microorganisms impact soil richness, to the glory of huge warm blooded animals molding scenes through their natural jobs.

Vegetation, as a basic part of biological systems, applies a significant impact on the setting. The variety of plant species, each adjusted to explicit natural circumstances, makes a mosaic of territories that help a wide exhibit of creature life. Backwoods, for instance, are not just characterized by the transcending trees that structure their covering yet additionally by the bunch of plant species that possess the understory. The layers of vegetation, from the woodland floor to the rising trees, give specialties to incalculable organic entities, molding the general biodiversity of the setting.

Photosynthesis, the cycle by which plants convert daylight into energy, lies at the core of the effect of vegetation on the setting. This inexplicable system supports the actual plants as well as structures the groundwork of the pecking order. Through photosynthesis, plants produce oxygen, a fundamental part for the breath of numerous organic entities, including people. The oxygen-rich environment made by plants plays had a pivotal impact in molding the tenability of Earth.

Notwithstanding their job as oxygen makers, plants are essential makers in food networks, giving food to herbivores and, accordingly, for carnivores in higher trophic levels. The presence of extraordinary plant species in a setting can hence decide the organization and wealth of creature life. In fields, the sort of grasses present impacts the herbivores that eat on them, from zebras in the African savanna to buffalo in North American grasslands.

Past their job in supporting food networks, plants add to the cycling of supplements in biological systems. Deterioration, worked with by growths and microorganisms in the dirt, separates plant material into natural matter, delivering fundamental supplements once more into the biological system. This supplement cycling is a key interaction that supports the wellbeing and efficiency of the setting.

In addition, certain plant species have novel variations that shape the actual attributes of the setting. Mangrove trees, for instance, flourish in seaside conditions with bitter water, making complex underground roots that act as nurseries for marine life. These seaside environments, molded by the presence of mangroves, give indispensable living space to different species, including fish and shellfish.

In bone-dry areas, delicious plants like desert flora have advanced water-putting away components to make due in water-scant conditions. Their presence characterizes the presence of desert scenes as well as gives a wellspring of hydration to abandon staying creatures. Creatures, for example, camels and rodents have advanced physiological variations to remove water from delicious plants, displaying the interconnectedness of plant and creature life in parched settings.

Exceptional plant transformations can likewise impact the fire systems in specific environments. A few plants have developed to flourish in fire-inclined conditions and even rely upon occasional flames for their propagation. The germination of specific tree species, similar to the famous goliath sequoias in California, is set off by fire, permitting them to lay out and fill in regions got free from contending vegetation.

Rather than the effect of vegetation, the presence of remarkable creature species adds to the natural elements and biodiversity of a setting. Creatures, as buyers and, at times, cornerstone species, assume essential parts in molding the design and capability of environments. The way of behaving and natural elements of creatures, from fertilization to seed dispersal, have broad ramifications for the setting.

Pollinators, including honey bees, butterflies, and birds, are fundamental for the proliferation of many blooming plants. Their job in moving dust between blossoms works with the preparation cycle, guaranteeing the development of seeds and the continuation of plant species. The vanishing of pollinators can have flowing consequences for plant populaces, influencing the food wellsprings of herbivores and the hunters that depend on them.

Seed dispersal, one more vital natural help given by creatures, adds to the spatial dissemination of plant species. Creatures that consume products of the soil assume a fundamental part in shipping seeds to new areas, advancing hereditary variety and the foundation of plant populaces in various regions. In tropical rainforests, where variety is especially high, the mind boggling connections between fruiting plants and their creature dispersers add to the perplexing embroidery of life.

Huge herbivores, for example, elephants and brushing ungulates, shape scenes through their taking care of ways of behaving. Their effect on vegetation can impact the organization of plant networks and make particular environments. For instance, the perusing exercises of elephants in African savannas can prompt the making of open meadows, influencing the overflow of woody vegetation and affecting the circulation of different herbivores.

Hunters, as hierarchical controllers of environments, impact the way of behaving and circulation of prey species. The presence of hunters can prompt changes in the taking care of propensities and spatial examples of herbivores, which, thus, influence vegetation elements.

The renewed introduction of hunters to specific environments, a training in preservation known as trophic rewilding, expects to reestablish natural cycles that have been disturbed by the shortfall of top hunters.

Cornerstone species, with unbalanced consequences for their biological systems, apply a critical effect on the setting. The expulsion of a cornerstone animal varieties can set off flowing impacts that echo through the whole environment. For instance, the renewed introduction of dim wolves to Yellowstone Public Park in the US significantly affected the way of behaving of elk, prompting changes in vegetation elements and in any event, adjusting the direction of streams.

The communications between novel plant and creature species frequently manifest in harmonious connections that add to the versatility of biological systems. Mutualistic beneficial interaction, where the two accomplices benefit, is exemplified by the connections between specific plants and mycorrhizal parasites. The organisms work with supplement take-up for the plants, while the plants give sugars to the growths. This mutualistic trade upgrades the supplement cycling and by and large soundness of the setting.

In coral reef environments, the advantageous connection between coral polyps and zooxanthellae, photosynthetic green growth, shapes the premise of the lively and various submerged scenes. The corals give a safeguarded living space to the green growth, and consequently, the green growth give the corals supplements through photosynthesis. This fragile equilibrium is critical for the development and upkeep of coral reefs, which support a heap of marine life.

Human exercises, nonetheless, have altogether modified the effect of remarkable plant and creature life on the setting. Natural surroundings obliteration, contamination, environmental change, and overexploitation present uncommon difficulties to the fragile equilibrium of biological systems. The deficiency of biodiversity, driven by these anthropogenic tensions, undermines the steadiness and working of environments around the world.

Deforestation, driven by the getting free from land for farming, logging, and metropolitan turn of events, has extreme ramifications for both plant and animal life. The obliteration of living spaces denies endless types of their homes, prompting populace declines and, at times, termination. The Amazon rainforest, frequently alluded to as the "lungs of the Earth," faces progressing dangers from deforestation, affecting the different vegetation as well as the heap of creature species that call this environment home.

The adjustment of normal fire systems, one more result of human exercises, can significantly affect environments adjusted to intermittent flames.

Smothering normal flames in specific conditions can prompt a gathering of vegetation, expanding the gamble of extreme and horrendous fierce blazes. The deficiency of plant species adjusted to customary flames can upset biological cycles and favor the foundation of obtrusive species.

Environmental change, driven by the outflow of ozone harming substances from human exercises, represents an inescapable danger to plant and creature life across the globe. Climbing temperatures, changes in precipitation designs, and the rising recurrence of outrageous climate occasions challenge the versatility of numerous species. Coral reefs, delicate to temperature changes, face the double dangers of fading and sea fermentation, jeopardizing the different networks that rely upon these environments.

Intrusive species, acquainted by people with new conditions, can outcompete local species for assets and upset laid out environmental connections. The spread of obtrusive plants, creatures, and microorganisms has prompted the downfall of local species in numerous settings. Islands, with their extraordinary environments and frequently separated biodiversity, are especially defenseless against the effects of obtrusive species.

Overexploitation of untamed life, driven by hunting, fishing, and the unlawful natural life exchange, compromises numerous species with termination. The interest for intriguing pets, conventional meds, and extravagance merchandise drives the unreasonable double-dealing of plant and creature assets. The poaching of famous species like elephants and rhinoceroses for their ivory and horns has driven these species to the edge of eradication.

4.2 Discuss how ecosystems contribute to the overall balance of the world.

Biological systems, the multifaceted snare of living organic entities and their actual climate, assume a critical part in keeping up with the general equilibrium of the world. These powerful frameworks, going from earthly backwoods to oceanic coral reefs, add to the strength of the planet by controlling environment, supporting biodiversity, cycling supplements, and giving fundamental biological system administrations. The relationship of living creatures and their current circumstance makes a sensitive harmony that supports life on The planet.

One of the central commitments of environments to the worldwide equilibrium is their part in controlling the World's environment. Through cycles, for example, photosynthesis and breath, plants and different creatures impact the groupings of ozone depleting substances in the environment. Plants retain carbon dioxide during photosynthesis, changing over it into oxygen, a fundamental part for the breath of numerous living beings, including people. Woods, specifically, go about as carbon sinks, sequestering a lot of carbon and relieving the effects of environmental change.

Past the immediate guideline of ozone harming substances, biological systems impact neighborhood and territorial environment designs. Backwoods, for instance, make microclimates by giving shade and delivering water fume through an interaction known as happening. This cooling impact can impact precipitation designs and add to the arrangement of mists. Wetlands, with their remarkable hydrological qualities, likewise assume a part in controlling neighborhood environment conditions by impacting water accessibility and temperature.

The biodiversity held onto inside biological systems is one more significant part of their commitment to the worldwide equilibrium. Biodiversity, the assortment of life on The planet, envelops the huge number of species, hereditary variety inside species, and the range of environments. The variety of species inside biological systems guarantees flexibility and versatility even with ecological changes. Every species, from microorganisms to dominant hunters, assumes an exceptional part in forming the construction and capability of environments.

The idea of cornerstone species represents the significance of specific species in keeping up with the respectability of environments. Cornerstone species lopsidedly affect their current circumstance, impacting the overflow and dissemination of different species. The evacuation of a cornerstone animal varieties can prompt flowing impacts, influencing the general equilibrium of the environment. Wolves in Yellowstone Public Park, for example, capability as cornerstone hunters, impacting the way of behaving of herbivores and, thus, molding vegetation elements.

Biological systems contribute fundamentally to the cycling of supplements, an interaction fundamental for the development and upkeep of living creatures. Supplement cycling includes the development of components like carbon, nitrogen, and phosphorus through the biotic and abiotic parts of environments. Decay, worked with by microorganisms, growths, and detritivores, separates natural matter into supplements that can be taken up by plants. This reusing of supplements guarantees the accessibility of fundamental components for the development of plants and, hence, for the creatures that rely upon them for food.

Wetlands, frequently alluded to as the "kidneys of the scene," are especially viable in supplement cycling. They channel and cycle water, eliminating abundance supplements and toxins before they arrive at downstream biological systems. Mangroves, beach front environments portrayed by salt-open minded trees, add to supplement cycling by catching dregs and separating supplements from the water. These environment capabilities are basic for keeping up with water quality and supporting the wellbeing of downstream living spaces.

Biological systems likewise give a large number of fundamental administrations that straightforwardly benefit human social orders. These environment administrations, frequently underestimated, incorporate the arrangement of clean water, fertilization of yields, guideline of bugs and infections, and the arrangement of food and unrefined components.

Wetlands, for instance, go about as normal water purifiers, separating contaminations and further developing water quality. Honey bees and different pollinators add to the fertilization of yields, guaranteeing the creation of natural products, vegetables, and other farming items.

Woodlands, notwithstanding their part in carbon sequestration, offer a bunch of biological system administrations. They give lumber and non-wood backwoods items, support biodiversity, manage water stream in waterways, and deal sporting and social qualities. The economical administration of timberlands is fundamental to guarantee the proceeded with arrangement of these administrations while keeping up with the general wellbeing of the environments.

Seaside environments, including mangroves, seagrasses, and coral reefs, offer vital types of assistance for waterfront networks. Mangroves go about as normal cushions, decreasing the effect of tempest floods and safeguarding beach front regions from disintegration. Coral reefs, frequently alluded to as the "rainforests of the ocean," support different marine life, offer open doors for the travel industry and amusement, and give livelihoods to a huge number of individuals who rely upon fisheries.

The general equilibrium of the world is unpredictably connected to the wellbeing and working of environments, and human exercises have progressively endangered these frameworks. Territory obliteration, driven by deforestation, urbanization, and rural development, upsets the complex connections inside environments and prompts the deficiency of biodiversity. Contamination, whether from modern overflow, farming synthetic compounds, or plastic waste, presents dangers to water quality and the wellbeing of amphibian environments.

Environmental change, driven by the consuming of petroleum derivatives and deforestation, is modifying the circumstances under which biological systems work. Climbing temperatures, changes in precipitation designs, and the rising recurrence of outrageous climate occasions present difficulties to the flexibility of numerous species. Coral reefs, delicate to changes in ocean temperature, face blanching occasions that undermine the mind boggling marine networks they support.

Overexploitation of normal assets, including overfishing and unlawful logging, exhausts environments of their ability to offer fundamental types of assistance. The deficiency of key species through hunting or fishing can upset environmental cycles, prompting lopsided characteristics in the overflow of different species. The downfall of dominant hunters, like sharks and enormous carnivores, can bring about expanded populaces of herbivores, influencing vegetation elements and possibly prompting environment debasement.

Protection endeavors, established in science, strategy, and local area commitment, are critical for shielding the general equilibrium of the world's environments. Safeguarded regions, for example, public parks and untamed life holds, give shelters to biodiversity and act as fundamental passages for the development of species.

Rebuilding drives plan to restore corrupted living spaces, once again introducing local species and advancing the recuperation of environments.

Economical administration rehearses, whether in ranger service, fisheries, or farming, are fundamental for guaranteeing the proceeded with arrangement of biological system administrations without compromising the wellbeing of environments. Supportable farming, for example, focuses on rehearses that limit natural effects, save soil wellbeing, and advance biodiversity. Accreditation programs, for example, those for economical ranger service and fisheries, assist customers with settling on earth cognizant decisions and backing mindful asset the board.

Worldwide participation is critical in tending to worldwide difficulties that rise above public boundaries. Arrangements and shows, for example, the Show on Natural Variety and the Paris Settlement on environmental change, give structures to nations to team up on the preservation and maintainable utilization of biodiversity and the alleviation of environmental change influences.

Neighborhood people group, frequently the stewards of regular assets, assume an essential part in the economical administration of biological systems. Native information, aggregated over ages, offers significant experiences into customary practices that advance conjunction with nature. Coordinating conventional environmental information with logical methodologies upgrades the adequacy of protection and reclamation endeavors.

Instruction and mindfulness raising drives are fundamental for encouraging a feeling of obligation and appreciation for the worth of biological systems. Ecological instruction programs, from schools to local area outreach, engage people with the information and abilities to settle on informed conclusions about their effect on the normal world. Interfacing individuals with nature ingrains a feeling of stewardship and elevates an aggregate obligation to safeguarding the general equilibrium of the world's biological systems.

4.3 Explore the symbiotic relationships between different species.

In the complicated woven artwork of Earth's environments, the harmonious connections between various species structure the underpinning of natural interconnectedness. These mind boggling unions, manufactured north of millions of years through the steady dance of development, weave a perplexing snare of relationship. From the minute to the lofty, each creature assumes a part in supporting the sensitive equilibrium of life on this planet.

One of the most antiquated and crucial instances of beneficial interaction is the connection among plants and mycorrhizal growths. Underneath the outer layer of the dirt, a secret universe of cooperation unfurls. Plant roots, looking for supplements, interweave with the multifaceted hyphal organizations of mycorrhizal parasites.

As a trade-off for the sugars delivered through photosynthesis, the parasites give the plant fundamental minerals like phosphorus and nitrogen. This underground organization isn't just a demonstration of the excellence of collaboration yet additionally a foundation of earthbound biological systems.

In the open seas, coral reefs stand as energetic submerged urban communities, clamoring with a bunch of life. The actual corals, frequently confused with rocks, are living creatures that structure a cooperative relationship with little green growth known as zooxanthellae. These green growth, dwelling inside the coral tissues, saddle the force of daylight to perform photosynthesis. Thus, they give the coral indispensable supplements, advancing their development and the arrangement of the complex designs that make up coral reefs. This mutualistic collusion isn't just urgent for the endurance of corals yet in addition upholds a whole environment of marine life that relies upon these energetic living spaces.

Birds and blossoming plants participate in a dance of mutualism that traverses mainlands. Through the course of fertilization, birds, for example, hummingbirds and honey bees move dust between blossoms, working with the propagation of innumerable plant species. Consequently, the birds get nectar, a sweet prize that energizes their high-energy ways of life. This complicated movement, sharpened by ages of co-evolution, exhibits the consistent joining of various life structures into an agreeable organic orchestra.

The African savannah, with its notorious occupants like zebras, wildebeests, and gazelles, features an exemplary illustration of mutualism among herbivores and birds. Oxpeckers, roosted on the backs of huge well evolved creatures, participate in a double job of advantageous interaction. They feed on ticks and different parasites that plague their hosts, giving a cleaning administration that benefits the two players. Consequently, the birds gain a feast and a portable roost that awards them a vantage highlight recognize likely hunters. This coalition is a demonstration of the versatile systems that rise up out of the consistent exchange between species in unique environments.

Underneath the transcending coverings of tropical rainforests, a maze of life unfurls. Subterranean insects and acacia trees share a mutualistic relationship that epitomizes the joined idea of biological associations. Acacia trees give sanctuary and food to insects as specific designs called domatia and nectar-delivering organs. Consequently, the savagely defensive insects act as watchmen, guarding the acacia tree from herbivores and contending plants. This complex coordinated effort shapes the construction of the timberland as well as features the multifaceted methodologies that arise when species become mutually dependent.

In the realm of microbial science, the human stomach harbors a clamoring local area of microscopic organisms, growths, and different microorganisms. This mind boggling environment, known as the stomach microbiome, assumes an essential part in human wellbeing.

The advantageous connection among people and these microbial occupants goes past processing, impacting parts of the insusceptible framework, digestion, and, surprisingly, psychological well-being. The many-sided balance among host and microorganism is a fragile dance that highlights the significance of keeping an amicable relationship for by and large prosperity.

Profound inside the sea profundities, aqueous vent environments uncover a world overflowing with life in apparently ungracious circumstances. Tube worms, shrimp, and different animals flourish around these vents, fed by the mineral-rich waters that regurgitate from the World's inside. Microbes, in a harmonious relationship with these vent-staying organic entities, convert synthetics from the vent discharges into energy through a cycle known as chemosynthesis. This astounding transformation exhibits life's strength and its capacity to track down food in the most surprising spots.

The complicated dance of hunter and prey is an unending topic in nature, molding biological systems through a sensitive equilibrium. The connection among wolves and elk in North American biological systems gives a striking illustration of how predation can impact the elements of whole scenes. As wolves apply hierarchical strain on elk populaces, the vegetation in these environments encounters an outpouring of impacts. Overgrazing diminishes, permitting the recovery of plant species and affecting the overflow and conduct of different creatures. This cascading type of influence, driven by the advantageous interchange among hunters and prey, highlights the sweeping outcomes of natural connections.

In the tiny domain, lichens exemplify a captivating coalition among parasites and green growth or cyanobacteria. These composite creatures, frequently found covering rocks and tree husk, grandstand a collaboration that benefits the two accomplices. The parasites give a defensive design and retain water and supplements, while the green growth or cyanobacteria contribute through photosynthesis. This amicable cooperation permits lichens to flourish in different conditions, from icy tundras to bone-dry deserts, featuring the versatility that rises out of harmonious connections.

The seas, immense and baffling, harbor unpredictable associations between species that shape the marine climate. Cleaner fish, for example, wrasses and gobies, structure advantageous associations with bigger fish by eliminating parasites and dead skin from their hosts. This cleaning administration not just advantages the cleanliness of the bigger fish yet in addition lays out a sensitive equilibrium in the marine environment. The cleaner fish gain a dinner while adding to the general strength of the local area, representing the relationship that describes life underneath the waves.

In the domain of agribusiness, people have tackled the force of advantageous interaction for centuries. The connection among harvests and pollinators, like honey bees, isn't just a characteristic peculiarity yet a basic part of horticultural efficiency. The mutualistic trade between blooming plants and pollinators guarantees the propagation of yields, adding to worldwide food security. Notwithstanding, this sensitive equilibrium faces difficulties in the advanced world, with factors like territory misfortune and pesticide utilize undermining the harmonious connections that support horticultural biological systems.

The advantageous interaction between nitrogen-fixing microbes and leguminous plants addresses a foundation of supplement cycling in earthbound environments. In particular root structures called knobs, these microbes convert barometrical nitrogen into a structure that plants can use. Consequently, the plants furnish the microbes with sugars as an energy source. This complex organization assumes an essential part in keeping up with soil fruitfulness and supporting the development of an extensive variety of plant species.

The perplexing connections among hunter and prey stretch out past earthbound biological systems to the endlessness of the vast sea. Orcas, or executioner whales, are dominant hunters that participate in multifaceted social designs and hunting systems. Their presence in marine environments impacts the dispersion and conduct of prey species, forming the elements of the whole food web. The transaction between these marine monsters and their prey highlights the perplexing associations that exist even in the apparently endless scopes of the ocean.

The infinitesimal domain of the rhizosphere, the dirt locale impacted by root emissions, is a focal point for harmonious connections. Mycorrhizal growths, microorganisms, and establish establishes participate in a perplexing dance that upgrades supplement take-up for plants and advances soil wellbeing. This subterranean cooperation is fundamental for the essentialness of earthbound biological systems, adding to the strength of plants despite natural difficulties.

The African savannah, with its famous occupants like zebras, wildebeests, and gazelles, features an exemplary illustration of mutualism among herbivores and birds. Oxpeckers, roosted on the backs of huge vertebrates, take part in a double job of beneficial interaction. They feed on ticks and different parasites that plague their hosts, giving a cleaning administration that benefits the two players. Consequently, the birds gain a dinner and a versatile roost that awards them a vantage highlight identify expected hunters. This partnership is a demonstration of the versatile techniques that rise up out of the steady transaction between species in unique environments.

Underneath the transcending shelters of tropical rainforests, a maze of life unfurls. Insects and acacia trees share a mutualistic relationship that embodies the interlaced idea of biological associations. Acacia trees give asylum and food to insects as particular designs called domatia and nectar-creating organs.

Consequently, the savagely defensive subterranean insects act as watchmen, guarding the acacia tree from herbivores and contending plants. This complex joint effort shapes the construction of the timberland as well as features the mind boggling techniques that arise when species become mutually dependent.

In the realm of microbial science, the human stomach harbors a clamoring local area of microscopic organisms, parasites, and different microorganisms. This complicated environment, known as the stomach microbiome, assumes a urgent part in human wellbeing. The cooperative connection among people and these microbial occupants goes past absorption, impacting parts of the invulnerable framework, digestion, and, surprisingly, psychological well-being. The many-sided balance among host and organism is a sensitive dance that highlights the significance of keeping an amicable relationship for generally speaking prosperity.

Profound inside the sea profundities, aqueous vent biological systems uncover a world overflowing with life in apparently unwelcoming conditions. Tube worms, shrimp, and different animals flourish around these vents, supported by the mineral-rich waters that heave from the World's inside. Microorganisms, in a cooperative relationship with these vent-staying life forms, convert synthetic compounds from the vent discharges into energy through a cycle known as chemosynthesis. This astounding variation exhibits life's flexibility and its capacity to track down food in the most surprising spots.

The mind boggling dance of hunter and prey is a never-ending subject in nature, forming biological systems through a sensitive equilibrium. The connection among wolves and elk in North American environments gives a striking illustration of how predation can impact the elements of whole scenes. As wolves apply hierarchical tension on elk populaces, the vegetation in these environments encounters a fountain of impacts. Overgrazing diminishes, permitting the recovery of plant species and affecting the overflow and conduct of different creatures. This cascading type of influence, driven by the advantageous interaction among hunters and prey, highlights the sweeping results of environmental connections.

In the tiny domain, lichens encapsulate an entrancing union among parasites and green growth or cyanobacteria. These composite organic entities, frequently found covering rocks and tree rind, grandstand a collaboration that benefits the two accomplices. The parasites give a defensive design and ingest water and supplements, while the green growth or cyanobacteria contribute through photosynthesis. This amicable coordinated effort permits lichens to flourish in various conditions, from cold tundras to dry deserts, featuring the versatility that rises out of harmonious connections.

The seas, immense and secretive, harbor mind boggling associations between species that shape the marine climate. Cleaner fish, for example, wrasses and gobies, structure advantageous associations with bigger fish by eliminating parasites and dead skin from their hosts.

This cleaning administration not just advantages the cleanliness of the bigger fish yet in addition lays out a sensitive equilibrium in the marine environment. The cleaner fish gain a dinner while adding to the general wellbeing of the local area, showing the relationship that describes life underneath the waves.

In the domain of farming, people have outfit the force of advantageous interaction for centuries. The connection among harvests and pollinators, like honey bees, isn't just a characteristic peculiarity however a basic part of horticultural efficiency. The mutualistic trade between blooming plants and pollinators guarantees the proliferation of harvests, adding to worldwide food security. Notwithstanding, this fragile equilibrium faces difficulties in the cutting edge world, with factors like living space misfortune and pesticide utilize compromising the cooperative connections that support horticultural environments.

The advantageous interaction between nitrogen-fixing microbes and leguminous plants addresses a foundation of supplement cycling in earthly environments. In particular root structures called knobs, these microorganisms convert air nitrogen into a structure that plants can use. Consequently, the plants furnish the microorganisms with sugars as an energy source. This unpredictable organization assumes a vital part in keeping up with soil ripeness and supporting the development of an extensive variety of plant species.

The complicated connections among hunter and prey reach out past earthbound environments to the tremendousness of the vast sea. Orcas, or executioner whales, are dominant hunters that participate in perplexing social designs and hunting methodologies. Their presence in marine environments impacts the dissemination and conduct of prey species, forming the elements of the whole food web. The transaction between these marine monsters and their prey highlights the many-sided associations that exist even in the apparently limitless scopes of the ocean.

The infinitesimal domain of the rhizosphere, the dirt locale impacted by root emissions, is a focal point for cooperative connections. Mycorrhizal growths, microorganisms, and establish establishes participate in a mind boggling dance that upgrades supplement take-up for plants and advances soil wellbeing. This subterranean joint effort is fundamental for the essentialness of earthbound biological systems, adding to the flexibility of plants even with natural difficulties.

The African savannah, with its famous occupants like zebras, wildebeests, and gazelles, features an exemplary illustration of mutualism among herbivores and birds. Oxpeckers, roosted on the backs of enormous vertebrates, take part in a double job of advantageous interaction. They feed on ticks and different parasites that plague their hosts, giving a cleaning administration that benefits the two players. Consequently, the birds gain a feast and a versatile roost that awards them a vantage highlight recognize possible hunters. This coalition is a demonstration of the versatile methodologies that rise up out of the steady exchange between species in unique biological systems.

Underneath the transcending shades of tropical rainforests, a maze of life unfurls. Insects and acacia trees share a mutualistic relationship that epitomizes the entwined idea of natural associations. Acacia trees give sanctuary and food to subterranean insects as particular designs called domatia and nectar-creating organs. Consequently, the savagely defensive insects act as gatekeepers, protecting the acacia tree from herbivores and contending plants. This complex cooperation shapes the design of the woods as well as features the multifaceted systems that arise when species become mutually dependent.

In the realm of microbial science, the human stomach harbors a clamoring local area of microscopic organisms, growths, and different microorganisms. This complicated biological system, known as the stomach microbiome, assumes a vital part in human wellbeing. The harmonious connection among people and these microbial occupants goes past assimilation, affecting parts of the invulnerable framework, digestion, and, surprisingly, emotional wellness. The mind boggling balance among host and organism is a fragile dance that highlights the significance of keeping an agreeable relationship for generally speaking prosperity.

Profound inside the sea profundities, aqueous vent biological systems uncover a world overflowing with life in apparently ungracious circumstances. Tube worms, shrimp, and different animals flourish around these vents, supported by the mineral-rich waters that regurgitate from the World's inside. Microorganisms, in a harmonious relationship with these vent-staying life forms, convert synthetics from the vent outflows into energy through a cycle known as chemosynthesis.

Chapter 5

Magic and Mysticism

Wizardry and otherworldliness have enamored human creative mind since days of yore, winding around their ethereal strings through the embroidered artwork of history and culture. Across different civilizations and ages, these slippery powers have been a wellspring of marvel, dread, and interest. Whether communicated through antiquated customs, mysterious practices, or fantastical stories, sorcery and enchantment have molded the manner in which social orders see the world and their place inside it.

The foundations of enchantment and magic broaden profound into the archives of mankind's set of experiences, interweaving with the earliest articulations of otherworldliness and the mission for figuring out the secrets of presence. In old civilizations, like Mesopotamia, Egypt, and Greece, people put stock in the impact of powerful powers that administered the universe. Ministers and priestesses filled in as go-betweens between the human domain and the heavenly, employing customs and chants to summon gifts or deflect catastrophes.

The old Egyptians, for example, held a significant faith in the supernatural properties of images and ornaments. Pictographs enhanced burial chambers and sanctuaries, each character conveying semantic importance as well as a strong otherworldly importance. The well known Book of the Dead, a manual for the hereafter, was loaded with mysterious spells planned to protect the spirit's excursion and guarantee a positive judgment before the divine beings.

In Greece, the Obscure Secrets and the Eleusinian Secrets were praised customs that guaranteed starts a more profound comprehension of the universe and the commitment of a favored the great beyond. These mysterious functions consolidated representative ceremonies, sacrosanct serenades, and symbolic lessons, cultivating a feeling of association with the heavenly and a higher plane of presence.

The Medieval times saw the ascent of speculative chemistry, a mysterious practice that tried to change base metals into gold and find the mixture of life. Chemists, like the incredible Hermes Trismegistus, mixed profound and material pursuits, seeing the change of metals as an illustration for the spirit's development. The perplexing imagery of catalytic texts and the quest for the savant's stone mirrored a mission for inward edification and the combination of the otherworldly and material domains.

During the Renaissance, a resurgence of interest in supernatural quality and the mysterious arose, prodded by a rediscovery of old texts and an intense interest in the recondite. Visionaries like John Dee, court crystal gazer to Sovereign Elizabeth I, dove into the magical components of math and tried to speak with celestial elements through intricate customs. The Airtight Request of the Brilliant First light, established in the late nineteenth hundred years, proceeded with this custom of mixing supernatural practices with mysterious insight.

Across the globe, native societies protected their own mysterious customs, frequently profoundly entwined with nature and the soul world. Shamans, worshipped as middle people between the physical and powerful domains, led customs to mend, divine the future, and keep up with agreement with the regular powers. In the Americas, the Local American medication haggle ceremonies of the Inca civilization epitomized a significant association with the grandiose request.

In Asia, the old Chinese idea of Qi, an energy force that courses through every single living thing, and the acts of Daoism and Confucianism embraced magical components. Taoist chemists looked for eternity through internal speculative chemistry, developing the solution of life inside the body. In the mean time, Indian enchantment tracked down articulation in the Vedas and Upanishads, investigating the idea of the real world, awareness, and the interconnectedness, everything being equal.

The middle age Islamic world was a pot of learning and development, where researchers like Ibn Arabi and Rumi dove into Sufism, an Islamic spiritualist practice. Sufi spiritualists participated in practices, for example, dhikr (recognition of God) and looked for an immediate, individual experience of the heavenly through profound discipline and examination.

The interchange between sorcery, mystery, and religion has been a complex and developing dynamic from the beginning of time. While a few strict customs consolidated supernatural practices, others censured them as sinful or as a type of magic. The Catholic Church, for example, wrestled with the strain between true precept and famous society customs that embraced otherworldly convictions. The witch preliminaries of the archaic and early current time frames exemplified the hazier side of this battle, as people, frequently ladies, were blamed for rehearsing noxious wizardry and confronted abuse.

The Period of Illumination in the seventeenth and eighteenth hundreds of years achieved a change in scholarly ideal models, stressing reason, science, and doubt. The ascent of observational request and the logical technique prompted the minimization of mysterious and enchanted viewpoints in the Western world. Be that as it may, this didn't stifle the charm of the obscure; all things being equal, it changed and adjusted to new intelligent flows.

The nineteenth century saw a restoration of interest in the mysterious, energized by the Heartfelt development and the interest with the baffling and the powerful. Figures like Madame Blavatsky, fellow benefactor of the Theosophical Society, advocated the possibility of old insight and magical information stowed away from the standard. The mysticism development, with practices, for example, seances and endeavors to speak with the soul world, built up momentum, giving a scaffold between the logical and the mysterious.

The turn of the twentieth century saw the development of new enchanted customs, frequently mixing components of Eastern mystery, Western otherworldliness, and mental bits of knowledge. Aleister Crowley, a questionable figure and a vital figure in the mysterious restoration, established the religion of Thelema and wrote works that consolidated formal wizardry, yoga, and otherworldly way of thinking. The impact of Crowley and different soothsayers saturated the nonconformity developments of the 1960s, where trial and error with changed conditions of cognizance and the quest for otherworldly significance crossed.

In writing, the topic of enchantment and supernatural quality has been a lasting wellspring of motivation. Legendary universes populated by wizards, magicians, and mystical animals have energized the creative mind of journalists and perusers the same. J.R.R. Tolkien's Center earth, with its captivated domains and strong relics, and J.K. Rowling's Wizarding World, where wizardry is an essential piece of regular daily existence, have become social standards that rise above simple amusement.

The class of imagination writing, with its foundations in old legends and fables, keeps on advancing, reflecting contemporary worries and investigating immortal topics. Creators like Neil Gaiman and Ursula K. Le Guin imbue their works with a nuanced comprehension of wizardry, involving it as a similitude to investigate the intricacies of human instinct, ethical quality, and the interconnectedness, everything being equal.

In film, the depiction of wizardry has gone through a comparative change, from early enhancements that passed a feeling of marvel on to complex visual narrating that investigates the mental and philosophical components of sorcery. Films as nolan Christopher's "The Distinction" dig into the contention among performers and the penances they make for their specialty, while Hayao Miyazaki's energized show-stoppers, for example, "Vivacious Away" and "Cry's Moving Palace," present mystical universes that challenge regular ideas of the real world.

The domain of sci-fi, while unmistakable from customary dream, frequently integrates components of wizardry or cutting edge innovation that line on the supernatural. Arthur C. Clarke's popular proclamation, "Any adequately cutting edge innovation is unclear from sorcery," highlights the obscured lines among science and the supernatural, recommending that the mission for information and understanding might itself at any point be a type of enchantment.

In contemporary society, wizardry and otherworldliness persevere in different structures, adjusting to the social and mechanical scene. New Age developments draw upon diverse sources, joining old insight, Eastern otherworldliness, and elective mending rehearses. The fame of practices like soothsaying, tarot perusing, and precious stone recuperating mirrors a cutting edge mission for significance and association with the extraordinary.

The web has turned into a virtual grimoire, a store of recondite information and a stage for the trading of supernatural thoughts. Online people group committed to mystery, agnosticism, and different mysterious customs associate professionals from around the world, cultivating a worldwide exchange on the idea of wizardry and its part in the 21st hundred years.

Logical progressions have not suppressed the human interest with the secretive and the unexplained. Quantum physical science, with its perplexing standards of trap and superposition, has been contrasted with otherworldly ideas, welcoming hypothesis about the interconnected idea of the real world. The investigation of awareness and the potential for mind-over-matter peculiarities keep on testing customary logical ideal models.

The resurgence of interest in hallucinogenics and their true capacity for actuating supernatural encounters has opened new roads for investigating changed conditions of cognizance. Research on the remedial advantages of substances like psilocybin and MDMA has gathered consideration, bringing up issues about the crossing point of science, otherworldliness, and the magical elements of human awareness.

Notwithstanding the variety of convictions and practices, the substance of wizardry and mystery lies chasing a more profound comprehension of the real world and the acknowledgment of an otherworldly, interconnected aspect past the ordinary. Whether communicated through old ceremonies, exclusive practices, or contemporary otherworldly developments, the journey for importance and the investigation of the mysterious stay characteristic for the human experience.

5.1 Introduce supernatural elements and their role in the world.

The world, as we see it from the perspective of our faculties and the structure of logical comprehension, is many times viewed as a domain represented by normal regulations and actual peculiarities. However, woven into the texture of the truth are strings of the extraordinary, components that resist the limits of the observational and challenge how we might interpret what is conceivable. These extraordinary features, going from mysterious powers to paranormal events, play had a critical impact in molding human convictions, societies, and stories over the entire course of time.

Otherworldly components can take heap structures, rising above the standard and presenting aspects past the extent of regular clarification. In legends and folklore, creatures like divine beings, spirits, and legendary animals exemplify the otherworldly, filling in as middle people between the human and heavenly domains. These substances frequently represent normal powers, feelings, or parts of the human condition, giving a system to understanding the mystifying and the otherworldly.

One of the prototype heavenly components found in different social customs is the idea of divine beings or gods. These strong creatures, whether living on Mount Olympus in Greek folklore, Asgard in Norse folklore, or the different pantheons of Hinduism, encapsulate parts of creation, obliteration, and the crucial powers that administer the universe. The connection among people and divine beings is frequently portrayed by customs, supplications, and legends that try to pacify or conjure divine blessing.

In polytheistic practices, the pantheon contains a different exhibit of divine beings, each with particular credits and spaces. For instance, the old Egyptian pantheon included Ra, the sun god; Isis, the goddess of enchantment; and Anubis, the lord of eternity. These divinities assumed basic parts in the existences of devotees, impacting regular peculiarities, directing moral standards, and giving a system to figuring out the secrets of presence.

Spirits, one more pervasive heavenly component, overcome any issues between the physical and magical domains. Found in animistic practices and native conviction frameworks, spirits occupy regular components, sacrosanct locales, and, surprisingly, ordinary items. The soul world is frequently viewed as interwoven with the material world, affecting the recurring pattern of life and filling in as watchmen or guides for the living.

In Japanese Shintoism, for example, kami are spirits that occupy regular highlights like mountains, waterways, and trees. These kami are loved and celebrated in customs, mirroring a profound regard for the otherworldly pith present in the normal world. Also, Local American societies trait profound importance to creatures, plants, and components, recognizing the interconnectedness of every single living thing.

Legendary animals, from winged serpents to unicorns, address one more feature of the heavenly. These fantastical creatures populate the legends of assorted societies, encapsulating both the fearsome and the great. Winged serpents, frequently tracked down in Eastern and Western fables, represent early stage bedlam, guardianship, or the equilibrium of restricting powers. Unicorns, then again, are frequently connected with immaculateness, magnificence, and slippery elegance.

Powerful components are not restricted to antiquated legends; they keep on pervading contemporary culture through writing, film, and famous creative mind. The dream type, specifically, has given a prolific ground to the investigation of the powerful. Works like J.R.R. Tolkien's "The Ruler of the Rings" and J.K. Rowling's "Harry Potter" series acquaint perusers with captivated universes packed with supernatural animals, spells, and journeys that rise above the limits of ordinary reality.

In writing, the extraordinary fills in as a vehicle for investigating complex subjects, from the idea of good and evil to the human condition. Gothic writing, with its accentuation on the puzzling and the horrifying, frequently includes extraordinary components that summon a feeling of wonderment and dread. Mary Shelley's "Frankenstein" digs into the outcomes of playing god through logical trial and error, obscuring the lines between the normal and the unnatural.

The job of otherworldly components reaches out past folklore and dream into strict customs. Wonders, divine intercessions, and prophetic dreams are vital parts of numerous religions, giving an otherworldly aspect to's how devotees might interpret the heavenly. In Christianity, the marvels credited to Jesus, like transforming water into wine or raising the dead, highlight the otherworldly part of the strict account.

Essentially, in Islam, the Quran is viewed as a phenomenal disclosure, and the existence of the Prophet Muhammad is set apart by otherworldly occasions, including the Night Excursion to the sky. These otherworldly events confirm the heavenly idea of the lessons and highlight the wonderful parts of strict confidence.

Paranormal peculiarities, like apparitions, hauntings, and clairvoyant capacities, address one more classification of powerful components that charm human interest. Across societies, accounts of ghosts and experiences with the powerful have been woven into the texture of fables. The faith in phantoms, fretful spirits of the departed, endures in different social practices and has filled innumerable stories of spooky places, memorial parks, and ghostly appearances.

In the domain of clairvoyant peculiarities, people guarantee to have extrasensory discernment (ESP), supernatural power, or the capacity to speak with the soul world. While cynics might excuse these cases as pseudoscience, the appeal of the paranormal continues, with progressing examinations and discussions encompassing the legitimacy of such encounters.

Present day innovation and the approach of the computerized age have acquainted new aspects with the investigation of the otherworldly. The web, with its immense storehouse of data and worldwide network, has turned into a stage for sharing paranormal encounters, leading virtual seances, and examining unexplained peculiarities. Online people group committed to the paranormal encourage a feeling of brotherhood among the individuals who try to disentangle the secrets past the shroud of the regular world.

The convergence of science and the extraordinary has yielded both doubt and interest. While logical request looks for observational proof and reasonable clarifications, certain peculiarities challenge the restrictions of current comprehension. Quantum physical science, with its puzzling standards of ensnarement and superposition, has been conjured to investigate the potential for interconnectedness past the traditional limits of reality.

The investigation of cognizance and adjusted conditions of mindfulness further hazy spots the lines between the normal and the otherworldly. Psychonauts and scientists the same investigate the impacts of hallucinogenics on discernment, cognizance, and magical encounters. The resurgence of interest in these substances has started conversations about their likely remedial applications and their ability to prompt significant, supernatural perspectives.

In mainstream society, the otherworldly keeps on enthralling crowds through TV programs, films, and vivid encounters. Otherworldly themed series, for example, "More abnormal Things" and "The X-Documents," mix components of sci-fi, frightfulness, and the paranormal to make stories that tap into basic feelings of trepidation and the charm of the unexplored world. These accounts frequently investigate the outcomes of experiencing the powerful and the effect of such encounters on people and society.

The job of the otherworldly in forming social stories reaches out to fables, metropolitan legends, and customs went down through ages. Stories of witches, vampires, and shape-shifters populate the aggregate creative mind, reflecting social tensions, moral illustrations, and the human interest with the strange and the illegal. The model of the legend's excursion, a story structure found in fantasies and legends around the world, frequently includes experiences with extraordinary creatures and difficulties that test the hero's grit.

The otherworldly likewise fills in as a figurative device for investigating mental and existential topics. The idea of the doppelgänger, a puzzling twofold or modify self image, shows up in old stories and writing as an image of struggle under the surface, the shadow self, or the results of moral decisions.

This theme, found in works as dostoevsky Fyodor's "The Twofold" and Edgar Allan Poe's "William Wilson," digs into the intricacies of character and the battle among light and obscurity inside the human mind.

5.2 Explore the rules of magic in the setting and its effects on the environment.

In the perplexing embroidery of fantastical universes and domains where sorcery holds influence, the guidelines overseeing its utilization are a key part that shapes the actual texture of presence. Enchantment, in these settings, is certainly not a whimsical power however a represented power with regulations and rules that direct its utilization and repercussions. Understanding the standards of enchantment in a given setting is vital, for it characterizes the limits inside which wielders of wizardry work and portrays the effect of their activities on the climate.

At its center, enchantment is many times depicted as a power that rises above the regular regulations overseeing the actual world. It can control reality, oppose gravity, and adjust the principal components that make up the universe. Nonetheless, this unfathomable potential is only sometimes without limitations. The principles of enchantment go about as a bunch of powerful regulations that guide its experts, forcing impediments that forestall misuse and keep a similarity to adjust in the fantastical domains.

One well known part of mystical frameworks is the idea of mana or mysterious energy. Mana fills in as the cash of sorcery, and professionals should attract upon this supply to project spells or perform otherworldly accomplishments. The renewal of mana may include different systems — reflection, customs, or taking advantage of normal wellsprings of otherworldly energy. The limited idea of mana presents an innate constraint, keeping spellcasters from unendingly employing boundless power and requiring vital and sensible utilization of their mysterious capacities.

Notwithstanding mana, the standards of sorcery frequently direct specialization and mastery. Wizardry is only occasionally depicted as a solid power; rather, it is partitioned into unmistakable schools or trains, each with its own arrangement of spells and applications. Experts might represent considerable authority in natural enchantment, magic, deception, or mending, among others. This specialization requires a profound comprehension of the picked school, and dominance frequently comes to the detriment of capability in other enchanted expressions. This acquaints an essential component with supernatural undertakings, as people should gauge the advantages of specialization against the flexibility of a more summed up approach.

Moreover, the standards of sorcery much of the time consolidate the guideline of comparable trade. This idea specifies that each mysterious activity has an equivalent expense or outcome. Whether it be a penance, an actual cost for the caster, or an accidental incidental effect, the possibility of comparable trade guarantees that enchanted includes some significant downfalls.

This standard adds profundity to mysterious stories, infusing a feeling of authenticity and outcome into the fantastical procedures. It likewise fills in as a moral and moral thought for characters, provoking them to gauge the possible implications of their otherworldly undertakings.

The climate wherein wizardry is polished assumes a critical part in forming the principles and results of supernatural use. In certain settings, the actual climate is a wellspring of supernatural energy, with ley lines, enchanted springs, or divine arrangements filling in as conductors for mana. Then again, certain conditions might be unfriendly to enchantment, delivering spellcasting troublesome or even dangerous. The interaction among wizardry and the climate makes a unique relationship that impacts the guidelines overseeing enchanted rehearses.

For example, a supernatural backwoods might enhance the powers of nature-based spells, permitting druids or nature mages to take advantage of the inactive energy of the environmental factors. On the other hand, a ruined no man's land might oppose mysterious control, requesting significant exertion and expertise from those endeavoring to project spells. The actual geology of the world, from mountains to seas, may hold onto interesting mystical properties that influence the adequacy and constraints of wizardry inside those locales.

Ecological elements can likewise impact the security and instability of mystical undertakings. A shaky otherworldly nexus, for instance, could cause erratic floods in enchanted energy, prompting unseen side-effects for spellcasters. The hour of day, periods of the moon, or divine occasions may likewise impact the strength of sorcery, adding a visionary aspect to the principles administering its utilization.

Besides, the effect of sorcery on the climate is an essential thought. The projecting of strong spells or the calling of mysterious elements might leave waiting impacts on the environmental factors. The dirt might become advanced or adulterated, vegetation could thrive or wilt, and the very air could gleam with remaining enchanted energy. This natural aftermath fills in as a visual sign of the strong powers at play, underscoring the interconnectedness of wizardry and the world wherein it unfurls.

In certain settings, the principles of sorcery direct that the abuse or abuse of mystical power can prompt a peculiarity known as otherworldly contamination. This idea places that wild projecting or the arrival of disastrous enchanted powers can corrupt the climate, making scourged scenes where life battles to flourish. The moral ramifications of otherworldly contamination frequently become focal topics in stories, as characters wrestle with the outcomes of their enchanted activities on their general surroundings.

The idea of mystical curios is another feature that interweaves wizardry with the climate. These articles, pervaded with powerful mystical properties, might be fundamental to the guidelines administering the supernatural framework.

From old books and captivated weapons to otherworldly gems, these ancient rarities frequently act as central focuses for mystical power, impacting the nature and extent of supernatural capacities. The mission for such curios can be a focal plot component, driving characters to explore misleading scenes, tackle enigmas, and stand up to imposing enemies to bridle or forestall the arrival of their mysterious energies.

In specific enchanted frameworks, the arrangement of people with various moral or moral codes might impact the strength and nature of their supernatural capacities. For example, a person sensitive to the powers of light and goodness could find their spells improved in big-hearted conditions yet reduced or upset in places saturated with obscurity or vindictiveness. This ethical aspect adds profundity to the account, as characters wrestle with outer foes as well as with the ethical compass that directs their supernatural activities.

The principles of sorcery additionally reach out to the transaction between supernatural creatures and the climate. In universes where fantastical animals, like mythical beasts, fae, or elementals, exist, their presence can shape the principles administering sorcery. A few creatures might be intrinsically receptive to explicit otherworldly components, filling in as channels or wellsprings of force. The association between enchanted creatures and the climate can prompt unions or clashes, and the actual presence of these animals might be predicated on the equilibrium of supernatural powers in their environments.

Condemnations and endowments are extra components that epitomize the standards of enchantment, especially corresponding to the climate. Reviled terrains might experience unending scourge or unnatural peculiarities, with the very earth dismissing the dash of life. On the other hand, favored terrains might prosper with overflow, where yields yield plentiful harvests and the air is injected with a feeling of imperativeness. These supernatural engravings on the climate add profundity to world-working as well as give story snares to characters leaving on missions to lift reviles or offer favors.

The arrangement of divine bodies, like moons, planets, or groups of stars, frequently includes noticeably in enchanted frameworks. Lunar stages, for instance, may impact the power of specific spells or the way of behaving of supernatural animals. Heavenly occasions, similar to shrouds or planetary arrangements, could proclaim the assembly of enchanted energies, opening old powers or opening passages between domains. The infinite part of wizardry presents a feeling of magnificence and mystery, binds the standards of sorcery to the heavenly dance of the universe.

5.3 Discuss how mystical elements contribute to the harmony or disruption of the world.

In the mind boggling dance between the enchanted and the unremarkable, the presence of otherworldly components in a fictitious or fanciful world turns into a strong power that can either encourage congruity or plant the seeds of disturbance. These mysterious components, whether encapsulated in supernatural powers, divine substances, or extraordinary peculiarities, assume an essential part in forming the equilibrium and elements of the world they occupy. From old legends to contemporary dream domains, the interchange of enchanted components fills in as a story support, driving the plot and investigating significant subjects of request, disorder, and the sensitive harmony between them.

One central manner by which mysterious components add to congruity in a world is by laying out a vast request or heavenly arrangement. In numerous fanciful and strict customs, divine beings or grandiose substances are portrayed as draftsmen of the universe, winding around an embroidery of presence with reason and plan. These creatures instill the world with a feeling of direction, a stupendous story that unfurls as indicated by heavenly will. The adherence to this vast request guarantees balance, with each magical component assuming an assigned part in keeping up with the congruity of the world.

For example, in antiquated Egyptian folklore, the divine beings exemplified regular powers and grandiose standards, for example, Ra addressing the sun and Ma'at representing vast equilibrium and equity. The customs and strict acts of the Egyptians were pointed toward lining up with these mysterious components, encouraging a feeling of request and soundness in both the human and heavenly domains. The congruity accomplished through the affirmation and arrangement with mysterious powers turned into a core value for cultural direct and administration.

In polytheistic customs, where different gods oversee different parts of presence, congruity is much of the time portrayed as the consequence of a sensitive equilibrium among these heavenly elements. The Greeks, for instance, trusted in the Olympian pantheon, with divine beings like Zeus, Poseidon, and Abbadon directing the sky, ocean, and hidden world, separately. The congruity of the world relied upon the participation and balance among these strong creatures, each adding to the astronomical request in their assigned space.

Then again, disturbance on the planet frequently emerges when otherworldly components go astray from their appointed jobs or when inestimable powers are tossed into disorder. This interruption can appear through the activities of insubordinate divinities, noxious extraordinary elements, or the abuse of mystical powers by mortal creatures. The results of such interruptions resound across the texture of the real world, prompting bedlam, catastrophe, and existential dangers to the world.

In Norse folklore, the idea of Ragnarok represents a calamitous occasion where vast request breakdowns, prompting a pattern of obliteration and resurrection. Loki, a prankster god, assumes a critical part in prompting disorder and friction, adding to the disentangling of the laid out concordance among the Norse divinities. The disturbance brought about by Loki's activities mirrors the delicacy of the enormous request and the potential for otherworldly components to influence the equilibrium towards commotion.

In numerous fantastical settings, the idea of a particularly favored one or forecasted legend frequently arises as a reaction to disturbances brought about by enchanted components. These picked people are bound to reestablish harmony and concordance by facing the pernicious powers or amending the results of supernatural wrongdoings. The legend's process turns into a story vehicle through which the enchanted and everyday domains cross, with the hero filling in as a channel for reestablishing balance.

The abuse of enchanted powers by mortal creatures is a common subject that adds to the disturbance of concordance in fantastical universes. Whether driven by arrogance, ravenousness, or perniciousness, people who employ supernatural capacities without regard for the guidelines and moral contemplations frequently become specialists of confusion. This subject is exemplified in the legend of Faust, where the eponymous person's settlement with Satan prompts unfortunate outcomes, displaying the risks of excessive supernatural pursuits.

Besides, enchanted components add to the interruption of the world when old predictions or illegal customs happen as expected. The opening of taboo information, the breaking of mysterious seals, or the enlivening of antiquated elements can release powers that resist the regular request. Lovecraftian writing, for instance, frequently investigates the outcomes of taboo information and the enlivening of vast detestations that oppose human perception, prompting existential dangers to the strength of the world.

The connection between enchanted components and the regular world is one more aspect through which agreement or disturbance is investigated. In settings where sorcery and nature are entwined, the maltreatment or disregard of the normal world can prompt desperate results. The fae society in Celtic folklore, for example, are portrayed as watchmen of nature, and their dismay with human infringement on normal environments can bring about hardship and disarray. On the other hand, when humans live together as one with mysterious components of nature, a cooperative relationship results, encouraging success and prosperity.

Interestingly, the double-dealing of otherworldly assets or the defilement of sacrosanct destinations frequently turns into an impetus for natural debasement and mystical lopsidedness. The exhaustion of otherworldly springs, deforestation of captivated forests, or the contamination of enchanted domains can set off a chain response of disturbances, influencing the supernatural components as well as the general concordance of the world.

This subject is reverberated in different old stories and dream accounts, stressing the interconnectedness of supernatural and normal powers.

The job of mysterious components in administration and cultural designs is a convincing viewpoint that adds to one or the other concordance or disturbance in fantastical universes. In settings where rulership is straightforwardly attached to divine heredity or otherworldly authenticity, the dependability of the domain relies upon the ruler's adherence to enchanted standards. The Ruler Arthur legends, for instance, portray the mission for the magical blade Excalibur and the heavenly right of the legitimate lord to employ it. The concordance of Camelot is unpredictably connected to the authenticity of Arthur's standard and his capacity to maintain the supernatural groundworks of his rule.

Alternately, when rulers or foundations exploit otherworldly components for evil purposes or disregard the direction of prophetic dreams, the outcome is many times political unsteadiness and social commotion. The idea of the "Frantic Lord" in dream writing, driven by dull supernatural impacts or adulterated by illegal information, delineates how the abuse of mysterious power at the most noteworthy echelons of society can prompt the disentangling of the social texture.

The subject of otherworldly components adding to agreement or disturbance is common in contemporary dream writing, where writers frequently investigate nuanced viewpoints on the outcomes of employing mysterious powers. In J.K. Rowling's "Harry Potter" series, for example, the supernatural world is depicted as an equal society with its own guidelines, organizations, and mysterious animals. The Service of Wizardry, entrusted with keeping up with supernatural rule of peace and law, addresses an endeavor to carry design and concordance to the otherworldly domain. In any case, the series likewise dives into the dim underside of mysterious governmental issues, investigating how debasement, bias, and the quest for power can disturb the amicability inside the wizarding scene.

The powerful between magical components and relational connections is another vital perspective that shapes the concordance or interruption inside fantastical universes. Love, companionship, and coalitions manufactured through enchanted bonds frequently become impetuses for positive change and the victory of good over evil. The force of kinship in defeating dim powers is a common theme in dream writing, underlining the groundbreaking and redemptive capability of certified associations between characters.

On the other hand, the breaking of collusions or the double-crossing of trust among characters with mysterious capacities can prompt inside dissension and outside dangers. The subject of the fallen legend, enticed by dull powers or headed to franticness by enchanted impacts, is a story prime example that investigates the potential for interruption inside the obligations of cooperation. This inner turmoil adds profundity to characters and highlights the ethical problems inborn in exploring the otherworldly domains.

The idea of predictions and fate is one more topical string that winds through fantastical stories, investigating how anticipated occasions and picked predeterminations add to the concordance or interruption of the world. Characters who wrestle with their forecasted jobs frequently face moral issues and existential difficulties, as the heaviness of predetermination conflicts with individual organization. The capacity to resist or satisfy predictions turns into an essential second that shapes the direction of the story and the destiny of the world.

The sensitive exchange among congruity and disturbance on the planet shapes the embodiment of innumerable stories, legends, and fantastical domains. This everlasting dance, frequently woven with strings of sorcery, enormous powers, and legendary elements, fills in as a story material that investigates significant subjects of equilibrium, disorder, and the multifaceted associations between the commonplace and the uncommon.

Congruity, with regards to these stories, appears as a condition of balance and request. It is a condition where the normal, heavenly, and cultural components combine consistently, making a reality where the powers that oversee presence work pair. This congruity can be encapsulated in different ways — enormous request directed by divine elements, a harmonious connection between otherworldly powers and nature, or a cultural construction that maintains the harmony between the mystical and the unremarkable.

One of the major articulations of concordance in fantastical universes lies in the idea of a grandiose or divine request. In numerous legends and strict customs, divine beings or enormous substances are depicted as engineers who have carefully planned the world, bestowing a fantastic reason to each feature of presence. These heavenly powers bring a feeling of direction and importance to the universe, laying out a story that unfurls as per their will. The adherence to this grandiose request guarantees soundness and equilibrium, making an existence where the mysterious and the unremarkable coincide in agreeable cooperative energy.

Polytheistic customs frequently portray concordance as the consequence of a sensitive equilibrium among different gods, each liable for various parts of presence. The Greeks, for example, ascribed the equilibrium of the world to the collaboration among divine beings like Zeus, Poseidon, and Abbadon. Every god had a space and a job to carry out, and their cooperation kept the grandiose control. This depiction highlights the interconnectedness of magical powers, recommending that the amicability of the world is dependent upon the harmony among these strong elements.

The connection between supernatural components and the normal world is one more aspect through which congruity is investigated. In settings where enchantment and nature are entwined, the arrangement between otherworldly powers and the climate becomes vital to the world's balance.

The idea of an agreeable concurrence among enchanted and normal components is exemplified in the guardianship of nature by supernatural creatures like the fae society in Celtic folklore. Their dismay with human infringement on regular living spaces fills in as an update that the equilibrium of the world relies upon the deferential connection between the magical and the normal.

In addition, the powerful between enchanted components and cultural designs contributes fundamentally to the depiction of agreement in fantastical universes. In domains where rulership is connected to divine heredity or mysterious authenticity, the strength of the domain depends on the ruler's adherence to enchanted standards. The Lord Arthur legends, for instance, grandstand how the congruity of Camelot is complicatedly associated with the authenticity of Arthur's standard and his capacity to maintain the mysterious groundworks of his rule. Cultural concordance in such settings is accomplished when rulers administer in arrangement with the supernatural rules that support their power.

On the other hand, cultural disturbance frequently emerges when supernatural components are disregarded, manhandled, or took advantage of for accursed purposes. In dream writing, rulers who disregard the direction of prophetic dreams or establishments that capitulate to defilement and abuse of mystical powers become specialists of bedlam. The idea of a "Frantic Lord" or undermined rulership shows how the dismissal for magical standards at the most elevated levels of society can prompt the disentangling of the social texture and the interruption of the world's congruity.

The double-dealing of supernatural assets or the despoiling of holy locales in fantastical universes can set off a chain response of disturbances, influencing the enchanted components as well as the general concordance of the world. The exhaustion of mysterious springs, deforestation of charmed forests, or the contamination of otherworldly domains are topical components that highlight the interconnectedness of mystical and regular powers. The results of such activities frequently manifest as ecological debasement, underscoring the delicacy of the harmony among enchanted and normal components.

Moreover, the arrangement of divine bodies frequently includes noticeably in the depiction of agreement in fantastical stories. Lunar stages, planetary arrangements, or heavenly occasions might impact the strength of specific spells, the way of behaving of enchanted animals, or the general equilibrium of otherworldly powers. This grandiose perspective presents a feeling of loftiness and enchantment, binds the standards of sorcery to the heavenly dance of the universe and adding to the general concordance of the world.

The subject of adoration, fellowship, and partnerships manufactured through magical bonds frequently turns into an impetus for positive change and the victory of good over evil. The force of kinship in beating dull powers is a repetitive theme in dream writing, underlining the extraordinary and redemptive capability of veritable associations between characters.

The bonds shaped through magical associations frequently act as an offset to problematic powers, supporting the story of congruity beating disarray.

Besides, the investigation of magical components and their commitment to relational connections is a urgent viewpoint that shapes the congruity or interruption inside fantastical universes. Characters who wrestle with their forecasted jobs frequently face moral dilemmas and existential difficulties, as the heaviness of fate conflicts with individual organization. The capacity to challenge or satisfy predictions turns into an essential second that shapes the direction of the story and the destiny of the world.

Then again, the breaking of coalitions or the disloyalty of trust among characters with otherworldly capacities can prompt inner dissension and outside dangers. The subject of the fallen legend, lured by dim powers or headed to franticness by mysterious impacts, is a story paradigm that investigates the potential for disturbance inside the obligations of partnership. This struggle under the surface adds profundity to characters and highlights the ethical issues inborn in exploring the otherworldly domains.

The results of magical wrongdoings, whether driven by arrogance, ravenousness, or vindictiveness, are in many cases depicted as troublesome powers that resonate across the texture of the real world. People who use mystical capacities without regard for the standards and moral contemplations become specialists of confusion, adding to the interruption of congruity. The abuse of otherworldly powers by mortal creatures is a repetitive subject that adds layers of intricacy to fantastical stories, underlining the risks of excessive mystical pursuits.

The powerful between otherworldly components and the common habitat is one more angle that impacts the depiction of congruity or disturbance in fantastical universes. Ecological elements can act as courses for otherworldly energy, with ley lines, mysterious springs, or heavenly arrangements going about as wellsprings of mana. The communication among wizardry and the climate makes a powerful relationship that impacts the standards overseeing mysterious practices and adds to the general congruity or interruption of the world.

In certain settings, the abuse or abuse of mystical power can prompt a peculiarity known as enchanted contamination. This idea proposes that careless projecting or the arrival of horrendous supernatural powers can pollute the climate, making cursed scenes where life battles to flourish. The moral ramifications of supernatural contamination frequently become focal subjects in stories, as characters wrestle with the results of their otherworldly activities on their general surroundings.

The job of mysterious antiquities likewise adds to the agreement or disturbance of the world in fantastical settings. These items, saturated with powerful mystical properties, might be fundamental to the standards administering the mysterious framework.

From antiquated books and captivated weapons to mysterious gems, these ancient rarities frequently act as central focuses for mystical power, impacting the nature and extent of otherworldly capacities. The journey for such curios can be a focal plot component, driving characters to explore tricky scenes, tackle enigmas, and face considerable enemies to outfit or forestall the arrival of their mysterious energies.

Chapter 6

Architectural Wonders

Engineering, an impression of human imagination and resourcefulness, has led to various marvels from the beginning of time. From old wonders that stand as demonstrations of the capacities of early civilizations to present day works of art that push the limits of plan, building ponders enthrall and motivate. This investigation takes us on an excursion across existence, divulging the narratives behind a portion of the world's most exceptional designs.

In the domain of old engineering, the Incomparable Pyramid of Giza remains as a persevering through image of Egypt's magnificence and persona. Worked around 2560 BCE, during the rule of Pharaoh Khufu, this monster structure is the biggest of the three pyramids on the Giza Level. Its exact development, utilizing gigantic limestone and rock blocks, keeps on astounding architects and history specialists the same. Speculations proliferate in regards to the techniques utilized by the old Egyptians, going from cutting edge numerical information to extraterrestrial help. No matter what the secret covering its creation, the Incomparable Pyramid stays a remarkable demonstration of the structural ability of old civilizations.

Moving toward the east to India, the Taj Mahal coaxes with its ethereal magnificence. Dispatched by the Mughal Ruler Shah Jahan in memory of his darling spouse Mumtaz Mahal, this ivory-white marble tomb is a show-stopper of Indo-Islamic design. Finished in 1653, the Taj Mahal agreeably mixes components from Persian, Ottoman, Indian, and Islamic structural styles. Its balanced format, complicated carvings, and the hypnotizing play of light on its surfaces add to its status as quite possibly of the most famous design on the planet.

In the core of Rome, the Colosseum remains as a demonstration of the magnificence of old Roman designing. Finished in 80 CE under Sovereign Titus, this enormous amphitheater could have more than 50,000 observers for gladiatorial challenges, creature chases, and false ocean fights. The Colosseum's creative plan, including a mind boggling arrangement of inclines, secret entryways, and lifts, worked with the quick and sensational organizing of occasions. Notwithstanding hundreds of years of rot and plundering, the Colosseum stays a strong image of Rome's compositional and social inheritance.

Abandoning the old world, the Hagia Sophia in Istanbul overcomes any barrier among relic and the archaic time. At first worked as a basilica in 537 CE by Ruler Justinian I, this design wonder later changed into a mosque under the Ottoman Realm and at last turned into an exhibition hall in 1935. The Hagia Sophia's huge vault, complicated mosaics, and transcending minarets mirror the combination of Byzantine and Ottoman engineering styles, making it an image of social union.

As we progress to the Renaissance time frame, Florence, Italy, arises as a center point of creative and design development. The Florence Church building, otherwise called the House of prayer of St Nick Maria del Fiore, remains as an incredible accomplishment of this period. Planned by Filippo Brunelleschi, the church building's notorious vault kicked off something new in designing and plan. Finished in 1436, Brunelleschi's vault stays the biggest brick work vault at any point developed, a demonstration of the Renaissance's obligation to pushing the limits of what was considered conceivable.

Wandering into the Ornate time, the Castle of Versailles in France typifies the plushness and glory related with outright governments. Developed under the reign of Louis XIV in the seventeenth 100 years, the castle's immense nurseries, resplendent insides, and the Corridor of Mirrors mirror the government's longing to feature its influence and riches. Versailles, with its careful plan and rich embellishments, remains as an image of the creative and compositional accomplishments of the Elaborate time frame.

Quick sending to the nineteenth 100 years, the Eiffel Pinnacle arises as a famous image of Paris and a demonstration of the potential outcomes of iron development. Planned by Gustave Eiffel for the 1889 Article Universelle, the pinnacle's cross section construction and taking off level tested ordinary ideas of engineering style.

At first met with doubt and analysis, the Eiffel Pinnacle has since become perhaps of the most conspicuous design on the planet, drawing in huge number of guests every year.

The twentieth century introduced a period of engineering trial and error and development. The Sydney Show House, planned by Jørn Utzon, exemplifies the mid-century innovator development. Finished in 1973, this compositional jewel on the shores of Sydney Harbor includes a progression of shell-like designs that make a particular and striking outline. The Sydney Show House's imaginative plan and designing deserve it UNESCO World Legacy status, cementing its place as a worldwide compositional symbol.

In the US, the Guggenheim Exhibition hall in New York City remains as a demonstration of the vision of planner Plain Lloyd Wright. Finished in 1959, the gallery's winding plan difficulties customary ideas of presentation space. The Guggenheim's consistent slope permits guests to encounter workmanship in a liquid, natural way, a takeoff from the compartmentalized exhibitions of traditional historical centers.

Wright's plan reasoning, known as natural design, is encapsulated in the Guggenheim, where structure and work flawlessly entwine.

The 21st century has seen a flood in cutting edge building plans that push the limits of what is possible. Dubai, a city inseparable from present day extravagance, flaunts the Burj Khalifa, the world's tallest structure. Planned by Adrian Smith of the building firm SOM, the Burj Khalifa takes off to a level of 828 meters, highlighting a smooth and current plan propelled by Islamic design. Its development required state of the art designing arrangements, including a supported substantial center and a tower that broadens the structure's level.

In China, the Bird's Home Arena in Beijing, planned by modelers Herzog and de Meuron, catches the creative mind with its perplexing and whimsical cross section like construction. Worked for the 2008 Summer Olympics, the arena's plan represents both the intricacy of present day designing and the interconnectedness of contemporary worldwide culture. The Bird's Home Arena remains as a demonstration of the job engineering plays in molding the personality of a city on the worldwide stage.

As we cross the globe, investigating compositional marvels that length hundreds of years, mainlands, and plan ways of thinking, it becomes apparent that these designs are not simply results of their time yet impressions of human goal, inventiveness, and mechanical headway. Each miracle recounts an interesting story, whether it be the old persona of the Incomparable Pyramid of Giza or the state of the art development of the Burj Khalifa.

These compositional ponders additionally act as markers of social personality and authentic importance. The Taj Mahal, for example, isn't just a demonstration of affection yet additionally an image of the Mughal Domain's imaginative accomplishments.

Likewise, the Colosseum remains as a persevering through image of Rome's strength and the scene that enraptured its residents. Along these lines, engineering ponders become interlaced with the stories of the civilizations that imagined them.

In addition, the development of structural styles and procedures reflects more extensive cultural changes. The change from the Gothic glory of the Florence Church to the sane straightforwardness of the Sydney Show House reflects the shift from middle age to present day sensibilities. Similarly, the change from the old style lines of the Parthenon to the inventive plans of the Guggenheim Gallery means a takeoff from custom and a festival of individual articulation.

Structural ponders likewise assume a vital part in forming metropolitan scenes and city personalities. The Eiffel Pinnacle has become inseparable from Paris, similarly as the Sydney Drama House characterizes the horizon of Sydney. These designs serve commonsense capabilities as well as become social images that reverberate with the two local people and guests the same. The horizons of significant urban communities all over the planet are characterized by the compositional marvels that beauty their points of view, becoming essential to the visual and social personality of these cities.

Notwithstanding their social and verifiable importance, building ponders frequently present specialized difficulties that stretch the boundaries of designing and development. The development of the Incomparable Pyramid of Giza, with its exactly cut stones and gigantic scope, stays a subject of discussion among researchers and specialists. The arch of the Florence Basilica, planned by Brunelleschi, expected imaginative answers for help its massive weight and accomplish remarkable level. The Burj Khalifa's transcending level required pivotal designing answers for endure wind powers and seismic action.

Mechanical headways play had a significant impact in molding the conceivable outcomes of compositional plan. The utilization of built up concrete in structures like the Sydney Drama House and the Burj Khalifa considers more prominent adaptability in plan and development. PC supported plan (computer aided design) and building data displaying (BIM) have changed the preparation and execution of compositional activities, empowering engineers to imagine and break down complex plans before development starts. These mechanical instruments have extended the innovative opportunities for engineers, permitting them to explore different avenues regarding unusual structures and materials.

The natural effect of compositional miracles has additionally gone under examination as of late. Feasible plan rehearses, like the utilization of inexhaustible materials, energy-proficient frameworks, and green rooftops, have acquired conspicuousness. The Nurseries by the Narrows in Singapore, with its notable Supertrees and manageable plan, represents a contemporary way to deal with blending compositional development with natural obligation.

As the world wrestles with environmental change and natural debasement, engineers are progressively integrating economical practices into their plans to limit the biological impression of new designs.

The social effect of building ponders is similarly critical. Public spaces like the Court de España in Seville or the Thousand years Park in Chicago act as get-together places for networks, cultivating social connection and social trade. Engineering miracles can likewise be strong images of political and social change. The Berlin Wall, when a disruptive hindrance, has changed into a material for creative articulation, representing the reunification of East and West Berlin.

As we ponder these compositional miracles, obviously they are not static elements frozen in time. Many have gone through changes and transformations to meet the changing necessities of society. The Hagia Sophia's progress from a basilica to a mosque and afterward an exhibition hall mirrors the perplexing history and social elements of the locales it has served. Essentially, the versatile reuse of modern designs like the Tate Present day in London as a contemporary workmanship historical center shows the limit of engineering to develop with the times.

The difficulties of the 21st 100 years, including fast urbanization, environmental change, and the requirement for supportable turn of events, present new contemplations for draftsmen. The idea of shrewd urban communities, coordinating innovation to upgrade metropolitan living, is forming the fate of metropolitan plan. Structures are turning out to be more energy-effective, with an emphasis on sustainable power sources and harmless to the ecosystem materials. The High Line in New York City, a raised park based on a previous rail route line, embodies the reusing of metropolitan foundation to make green spaces that improve the personal satisfaction for city tenants.

Taking everything into account, design ponders are not just designs of stone, cement, or steel; they are exemplifications of human goals, impressions of social characters, and demonstrations of the advancement of progress. From the old wonders that oppose clarification to the contemporary designs that push the limits of plan, each building wonder recounts an account of resourcefulness, inventiveness, and the steadily developing connection among mankind and its constructed climate. As we keep on wondering about these miracles and witness the introduction of new building works of art, we are helped that the language to remember engineering is an all inclusive one, addressing the common dreams and desires of humankind across existence.

6.1 Highlight the significance of architecture in world-building.

Engineering, past being a practical need, is a significant articulation of human inventiveness that shapes the physical and social scenes of our reality. Its importance stretches out a long ways past simple designs; it is an essential component in the specialty of world-building, impacting social orders, molding personalities, and making a permanent imprint on the human experience.

At its center, design is the unmistakable sign of the qualities, convictions, and desires of a general public. Think about the Gothic churches of archaic Europe, like Notre-Lady in Paris. These transcending structures were not simply places of love but rather likewise images of the profound and fleeting force of the Congregation. The complicated subtleties of their plan, from the taking off towers to the fragile lattice of stained glass windows, conveyed a feeling of heavenly loftiness and human commitment.

Along these lines, the mosques of Islamic engineering, similar to the Alhambra in Spain or the Blue Mosque in Istanbul, act as exemplifications of social and strict personality. The mathematical examples, mind boggling calligraphy, and luxurious vaults convey an agreeable mix of profound importance and imaginative greatness. Through design, these designs become the actual portrayal of a development's qualities and a demonstration of its social accomplishments.

Design likewise assumes a urgent part in forming the stories of urban communities and countries. The horizons of significant cities, characterized by famous designs like the Eiffel Pinnacle in Paris or the Burj Khalifa in Dubai, become visual images that epitomize the substance of a spot. The juxtaposition of verifiable and current design in a cityscape recounts an account of development, mirroring the changing elements of society and the progression of time.

Think about the city of Rome, where old marvels like the Colosseum and the Roman Gathering stand one next to the other with Renaissance castles and Elaborate temples. This building embroidery winds around together the strings of history, displaying the layers of social and political impacts that have molded the Everlasting City.

Each building turns into a part in the story of Rome, adding to its special person and worldwide importance.

The meaning of engineering in world-building isn't restricted to the domain of actual designs; it reaches out to the making of fictitious universes in writing and film. In works of imagination and sci-fi, planners use an exceptional type of story power. J.R.R. Tolkien, in his making of Center earth, utilized design for the purpose of narrating. The transcending towers of Minas Tirith and the supernatural lobbies of Rivendell are not simply settings but rather indispensable components that convey the set of experiences, culture, and legend of Tolkien's made up domain.

Additionally, the wizarding universe of Harry Potter, rejuvenated by J.K. Rowling, highlights design that rises above simple foundation view. Hogwarts School of Black magic and Wizardry, with its moving flights of stairs and captivated rooms, turns into a person by its own doing. The mystical design of Diagon Rear entryway and the premonition construction of Azkaban Jail add to the vivid experience of Rowling's fantastical universe, adding layers of profundity to the account.

In the domain of film, the tragic cityscapes of "Cutting edge Sprinter" and "City" are visual scenes as well as essential parts of the narrating system. The transcending megastructures and neon-lit streetscapes convey a feeling of severe futurism, establishing the vibe for the stories of these tragic universes. The design turns into a quiet person, impacting the mind-set and environment of the story.

Design's part in world-building is maybe most clear in the domain of computer games. In virtual universes, draftsmen assume the job of divine beings, forming whole scenes and human advancements. Games like "Minecraft" permit players to become engineers of their own universes, building everything from basic houses to expound palaces. The game's blocky tasteful turns into a material for players to communicate their inventiveness and creative mind, featuring the democratizing force of design in the computerized domain.

More refined models incorporate games like "Professional killer's Ideology," where verifiable urban communities like Renaissance Florence and old Rome are fastidiously reproduced. The degree of detail in these virtual conditions serves as a setting for ongoing interaction as well as a type of intuitive schooling, permitting players to investigate and draw in with verifiable design in manners that conventional media can't imitate.

The design decisions in computer games additionally impact ongoing interaction mechanics and story advancement. The format of a city, the plan of a palace, or the construction of a spaceship can all effect how players explore and encounter the virtual world. Along these lines, design turns into a device for molding the visual feel as well as the actual texture of the game world and the tales that unfurl inside it.

Getting back to the actual world, the plan of public spaces and metropolitan arranging significantly impacts social elements and local area collaborations. Consider the effect of all around planned public squares like Piazza San Marco in Venice or

Times Square in New York City. These spaces, molded by structural choices, become center points of social trade, parties, and city character.

Conversely, ineffectively planned metropolitan spaces can add to social seclusion and separation. The idea of "endless suburbia," portrayed by low-thickness, vehicle subordinate turn of events, frequently brings about divided networks and an absence of energetic public spaces. Engineering, when drawn closer with aversion to human requirements and local area elements, has the ability to encourage social union and establish conditions where individuals can flourish.

Besides, engineering is a language of inclusivity or rejection. The plan of public structures, transportation frameworks, and foundation can either work with or upset admittance for people with assorted capacities. The idea of all inclusive plan, which expects to establish conditions that are open to individuals of all capacities and incapacities, highlights the social obligation of engineers to think about the requirements of the whole local area.

With regards to maintainability, design assumes a critical part in tending to the ecological difficulties within recent memory. The plan and development of structures represent a critical piece of energy utilization and ozone depleting substance emanations. As the world wrestles with environmental change, modelers are progressively embracing feasible plan rehearses.

Green structure advancements, energy-effective plans, and the utilization of sustainable materials are becoming standard contemplations in engineering projects. The idea of "biophilic plan," which tries to incorporate regular components into assembled conditions, improves the stylish allure of spaces as well as advances prosperity and ecological stewardship.

Engineering advancements like green rooftops, which integrate living vegetation into building structures, add to energy productivity and metropolitan biodiversity. Likewise, the idea of "aloof plan" uses regular components, for example, daylight and twist to manage temperature and diminish the dependence on counterfeit warming and cooling frameworks.

The compositional local area is likewise investigating the capability of reusing existing designs as a reasonable option in contrast to new development. Versatile reuse, as found in projects like the High Line in New York City or the Tate Present day in London, jelly social legacy as well as limits the natural effect of obliterating and revamping.

As our reality wrestles with the difficulties of fast urbanization, environmental change, and social disparity, the job of design in world-building takes on significantly more noteworthy importance. Modelers are not simple originators of spaces; they are visionaries who shape the eventual fate of our urban communities and networks. Their decisions concerning plan, materials, and usefulness have sweeping ramifications for the prosperity of people, the strength of the planet, and the social structure holding the system together.

All in all, the meaning of design in world-building is complex and significant. From the fantastic houses of God of middle age Europe to the cutting edge cityscapes of sci-fi, design is a language that addresses the spirit of humankind. It shapes our actual surroundings, impacts our social personalities, and fills in as a material for narrating in writing, film, and computer games.

In the contemporary world, modelers bear a significant obligation as stewards of the constructed climate. Their choices influence the style of our urban areas as well as the personal satisfaction, the inclusivity of spaces, and the maintainability of our networks. As we explore the intricacies of the 21st 100 years, the job of design in world-building turns into a urgent focal point through which we can imagine a future that is both utilitarian and lovely, feasible and spectacular.

6.2 Explore how different civilizations shape their environments through buildings.

The constructed climate, formed by building tries, fills in as a substantial impression of the qualities, convictions, and needs of various civilizations since forever ago. The manners by which social orders develop their structures and metropolitan scenes are not simply practical necessities but rather conscious articulations of social character, cultural designs, and mechanical capacities. By looking at the building accomplishments of different developments, we can disentangle the multifaceted connection among individuals and their assembled environmental factors.

Old Egypt, with its persevering through progress along the banks of the Nile, gives a convincing beginning stage. The pyramids of Giza, especially the Incomparable Pyramid, stand as notable designs that have spellbound human creative mind for centuries. Built around 2560 BCE during the rule of Pharaoh Khufu, the Incomparable Pyramid is a demonstration of the old Egyptians' high level designing abilities. The accuracy with which huge limestone and rock blocks were quarried, moved, and gathered difficulties contemporary understandings of the innovative abilities of the time. The pyramids served as burial chambers for pharaohs as well as images of heavenly power and perpetual quality, mirroring the Egyptians' convictions in a the hereafter and their craving to deify their rulers.

In old Greece, the Parthenon, roosted on the Acropolis in Athens, remains as a getting through image of traditional design and the beliefs of the city-state. Underlying the fifth century BCE, the Parthenon is a Doric sanctuary devoted to the goddess Athena. Its plan, credited to the modeler Iktinos and the artist Phidias, exemplifies the standards of Greek design with its agreeable extents and accentuation on balance. The friezes and models that embellished the Parthenon portrayed fanciful accounts and commended the social and political accomplishments of Athens. The compositional dominance and imaginative embellishments of the Parthenon mirrored the upsides of popularity based administration and the quest for scholarly and stylish greatness that characterized old Greece.

Moving toward the east to old Rome, the Colosseum arises as a great demonstration of Roman designing and the display of public diversion. Finished in 80 CE under Sovereign Titus, the Colosseum could oblige more than 50,000 onlookers for gladiatorial challenges, creature chases, and counterfeit ocean fights. Its imaginative plan, including a perplexing arrangement of slopes, hidden entryways, and lifts, took into consideration quick and sensational organizing of occasions. The Colosseum, with its excellent curves and huge scope, mirrored the may and greatness of the Roman Domain, turning into an image of supreme power and city pride.

In the Byzantine Domain, the Hagia Sophia in Constantinople (current Istanbul) arose as a work of art of engineering development. Worked under Head Justinian I in 537 CE, the Hagia Sophia exhibited the progress from old style Roman design to Byzantine feel.

The tremendous vault, upheld by pendentives, made a feeling of weightlessness and otherworldly greatness. The complicated mosaics that decorated the inside conveyed strict accounts and accentuated the association between the natural and the heavenly. The Hagia Sophia, at first a house of prayer, later changed over into a mosque, and in the end an exhibition hall, exemplified the social and strict development of the Byzantine Realm.

As we cross mainlands and ages, Islamic engineering turns into an entrancing focal point through which to investigate the transaction of social, strict, and stylish contemplations. The Alhambra in Granada, Spain, worked in the thirteenth 100 years by the Nasrid line, embodies the wonderful excellence of Islamic craftsmanship and engineering. The perplexing elements multifaceted mathematical examples, arabesques, and calligraphy, making a visual embroidery that mirrors the Islamic accentuation on solidarity, balance, and the heavenly. The Alhambra, with its yards, gardens, and resplendent royal residences, filled in as an actual sign of the Islamic idea of heaven on the planet.

In South Asia, the Taj Mahal in Agra, India, is a quintessential illustration of Mughal design. Dispatched by Head Shah Jahan in the seventeenth 100 years as a catacomb for his cherished spouse Mumtaz Mahal, the Taj Mahal epitomizes the combination of Persian, Ottoman, Indian, and Islamic compositional styles. The even design, unpredictable marble trim work, and the famous white vault add to its status as a worldwide engineering wonder. The Taj Mahal, with its ethereal magnificence, mirrors the Mughal accentuation on glory, love, and imaginative greatness.

The archaic period in Europe saw the ascent of Gothic engineering, portrayed by taking off basilicas with pointed curves, ribbed vaults, and flying braces. The Church of Notre-Lady in Paris, started in the twelfth 100 years, embodies the Gothic style and fills in as a zenith of French Gothic design. The utilization of creative underlying components took into account sweeping stained glass windows, for example, the well known rose windows, which overflowed the inside with light and variety. Notre-Woman, with its glorious pinnacles and mind boggling figures, turned into a profound and social focus, mirroring the middle age Christian perspective and the significance of heavenly light.

The Renaissance in Italy denoted a restoration of old style standards and a recharged interest in humanism. Florence, the focal point of this social renaissance, flaunts compositional show-stoppers that exemplify the time's scholarly and creative mature. The Florence Church building, or the House of God of St Nick Maria del Fiore, remains as an unparalleled accomplishment of Renaissance design. Planned by Filippo Brunelleschi, the church building's notable arch kicked off something new in designing and plan. Finished in 1436, the vault stays the biggest brick work arch at any point built, a demonstration of the Renaissance's obligation to pushing the limits of what was considered conceivable.

Wandering into the Ornate time frame, the Castle of Versailles in France typifies the extravagance and glory related with outright governments. Built under the reign of Louis XIV in the seventeenth hundred years, the royal residence's immense nurseries, elaborate insides, and the Corridor of Mirrors mirror the government's craving to exhibit its influence and riches. Versailles, with its fastidious plan and extravagant embellishments, remains as an image of the imaginative and compositional accomplishments of the Elaborate time frame.

The nineteenth century saw the ascent of industrialization and the appearance of new materials and development methods. The Gem Royal residence in London, planned by Joseph Paxton for the Incomparable Display of 1851, epitomized the soul of development and advancement. The design, made of iron and glass, displayed the conceivable outcomes of construction and large scale manufacturing. The Precious stone Royal residence, with its extensive inside and straightforward walls, represented the confidence of the Modern Transformation and the potential for human advancement through innovation.

In the US, the late nineteenth and mid twentieth hundreds of years considered the rise of the high rise to be a quintessential type of American design. The Flatiron Working in New York City, finished in 1902, is a perfect representation of early high rise plan. Obliged by its three-sided plot, the structure rises emphatically, testing conventional thoughts of engineering structure. The Flatiron Working, with its Beaux-Expressions enumerating, turned into a notorious image of the city's horizon and a forerunner to the transcending high rises that would characterize metropolitan scenes in the a long time to come.

The twentieth century introduced a time of structural trial and error and development. Innovator engineers, like Le Corbusier and Honest Lloyd Wright, tried to split away from verifiable styles and embrace a new, useful tasteful. The Bauhaus development, established in Germany in 1919, stressed the joining of workmanship, specialty, and innovation in building plan. The Bauhaus school, drove by Walter Gropius, impacted an age of planners with its obligation to effortlessness, usefulness, and the utilization of modern materials.

In the US, the mid-twentieth century saw the advancement of the Global Style, portrayed by clean lines, negligible ornamentation, and an accentuation on usefulness. The Seagram Working in New York City, planned by Ludwig Mies van der Rohe and Philip Johnson, turned into a milestone of the Global Style. With its smooth glass exterior and creative utilization of steel, the Seagram Building exemplified the standards of pioneer engineering and the ethos of the post bellum period.

As we approach the contemporary time, design has become progressively different, mirroring a pluralistic methodology that integrates components from different verifiable periods and social customs. The Sydney Show House, planned by Jørn Utzon and finished in 1973, remains as a famous image of Australia's social character.

Its sail-like designs, propelled by natural structures, make a striking outline against the Sydney Harbor. The Sydney Drama House, with its creative plan and designing, represents the combination of imaginative articulation and mechanical ability in the late twentieth hundred years.

The 21st century has seen a flood in vanguard engineering plans that push the limits of what is possible. In Dubai, the Burj Khalifa, planned by Adrian Smith of the design firm SOM, remains as the world's tallest structure. Finished in 2010, the Burj Khalifa takes off to a level of 828 meters, highlighting a smooth and present day plan enlivened by Islamic design. Its development required state of the art designing arrangements, including a supported substantial center and a tower that broadens the structure's level. The Burj Khalifa, with its cutting edge stylish, epitomizes the contemporary way to deal with compositional plan and the aspiration to make structures that oppose regular cutoff points.

6.3 Discuss the impact of architectural choices on the overall harmony of the setting.

Building decisions employ a significant impact on the general congruity of a setting, forming the visual and experiential parts of the constructed climate. Whether in verifiable landmarks, contemporary cityscapes, or fictitious universes, the choices made by designers and metropolitan organizers reverberate a long ways past the underlying domain, influencing the mind-set, usefulness, and social personality of a space. This investigation digs into the diverse manners by which engineering decisions add to or disturb the general congruity of a setting.

The idea of congruity in engineering reaches out past simple tasteful contemplations; it envelops a comprehensive equilibrium that coordinates structure and capability, culture and setting, and individual components into a strong entirety. Verifiable models, like the Parthenon in old Greece, embody the quest for engineering congruity. Planned by Iktinos and Phidias in the fifth century BCE, the Parthenon's old style extents, utilization of the Doric request, and regard for balance make a feeling of harmony and visual cognizance. The design decisions made in the Parthenon mirror the philosophical standards of old Greece, where the quest for equilibrium and concordance stretched out to both the physical and scholarly domains.

Moving to the domain of metropolitan preparation, the city of Rome gives an informative illustration of how structural decisions shape the congruity of a setting. The Renaissance overhaul of Rome, led by Pope Sixtus V in the late sixteenth 100 years, expected to upgrade the city's visual and spatial soundness. The execution of fantastic tomahawks, wide streets, and great wellsprings, for example, the famous Fontana di

Trevi, changed the turbulent middle age city into an organized and amicable metropolitan scene. The design decisions made during this period not just mirrored the power and desires of the Catholic Church yet in addition added to the production of a city that resounded with a feeling of request and solidarity.

Conversely, design decisions can likewise be troublesome, prompting an absence of congruity in the fabricated climate. Endless suburbia, described by low-thickness improvement, far reaching parking garages, and disengaged areas, epitomizes a take-off from amicable metropolitan preparation. This example, frequently determined via auto driven plan standards, adds to natural debasement, social seclusion, and an absence of firm character inside metropolitan regions. decisions for individualized portability and rural extension, while tending to specific requirements, upset the congruity of the generally metropolitan setting.

The effect of building decisions on amicability turns out to be significantly more articulated with regards to social character. The Taj Mahal in Agra, India, remains as a model of design amicability that rises above simple stylish contemplations. Worked by Sovereign Shah Jahan in the seventeenth hundred years as a sepulcher for his cherished spouse Mumtaz Mahal, the Taj Mahal consolidates components of Persian, Ottoman, and Indian compositional styles. The white marble structure, decorated with many-sided flower themes and calligraphy, mirrors the Mughal combination of assorted social impacts. structural decisions in the plan of the Taj Mahal fit with the social and strict upsides of the Mughal Realm, making a landmark that typifies both quality and otherworldly importance.

Then again, cases where engineering decisions conflict with social setting can prompt disharmony. The burden of Western building styles in non-Western settings during times of colonization represents this strife. The juxtaposition of neoclassical European structures in the core of urban communities in Africa, Asia, or the Americas frequently brought about a visual cacophony, as these designs didn't resound with the social, climatic, or context oriented states of their environmental elements. The conflict between compositional decisions established in frontier desires and the native social texture made a discernible feeling of disharmony, mirroring the power elements and social lopsided characteristics of the time.

Inspecting the effect of design decisions on concordance requires an investigation of how individual structures add to the intelligibility of a cityscape. In Paris, the structural decisions made during the rule of Napoleon III and his metropolitan organizer Georges-Eugène Haussmann changed the city into a model of metropolitan concordance. The excellent lanes, uniform structure exteriors, and public squares made a feeling of request and visual congruity. The compositional decisions, like the utilization of Haussmannian limestone exteriors and uniform structure levels, expected to upgrade the stylish solidarity of the city. This intentional arranging system addressed functional contemplations as well as added to the making of an agreeable metropolitan character that perseveres right up 'til now.

In any case, engineering decisions can likewise upset the congruity of a cityscape when they focus on uniqueness over context oriented joining. The unrestrained multiplication of high rises in a few contemporary metropolitan settings, driven by a longing for famous tourist spots and business practicality, can bring about an absence of visual attachment.

The juxtaposition of dissimilar engineering styles and scales might prompt a horizon that comes up short on agreeable stream and congruity found in urban communities with more controlled and logical preparation. This quest for singularity can incidentally upset the general concordance of the metropolitan climate, lessening the visual lucidness and social personality of the city.

In the domain of fictitious universes, structural decisions assume a significant part in laying out the general congruity of a setting. J.K. Rowling's portrayal of Hogwarts School of Black magic and Wizardry in the Harry Potter series fills in as an illustrative model. The assorted design styles, captivated highlights, and otherworldly components of Hogwarts add to the general amicability of the wizarding scene. From the moving flights of stairs to the transcending towers of the palace, each engineering decision lines up with the fantastical idea of the story, making a setting that resounds with a feeling of marvel and union. conscious decisions in the plan of Hogwarts add to the vivid experience of the made up world, upgrading the general congruity of the account.

On the other hand, the disharmony in design decisions can be purposely utilized to convey explicit account subjects. In tragic settings, for example, the cutting edge cityscapes portrayed in films like "Sharp edge Sprinter," the engineering decisions underscore disharmony, rot, and a feeling of severe futurism. The transcending megastructures, rambling neon-lit streetscapes, and juxtaposition of old and new building components make an environment of strife. This deliberate disturbance of design congruity fills in as a visual similitude for the tragic stories, reflecting cultural rot, mechanical overabundance, and the outcomes of uncontrolled urbanization.

Getting back to this present reality, the effect of building decisions on congruity turns out to be especially clear in the plan of public spaces. The idea of placemaking, which underlines the production of conditions that cultivate social communication and a feeling of local area, depends intensely on insightful engineering decisions. Public squares like Piazza San Marco in Venice or Court City hall leader in Madrid epitomize how compositional choices can add to the general congruity of a space. The selection of materials, the plan of seating, the combination of vegetation, and the presence of compositional tourist spots all assume a part in molding the climate and usefulness of these public spaces.

Conversely, ineffectively planned public spaces can prompt disharmony and an absence of municipal commitment. Spaces that focus on vehicular traffic over common cordial plan, or that need welcoming components like seating, lighting, and public workmanship, may beat local area communication down. The engineering decisions made in the plan of public spaces impact the social elements, inclusivity, and generally speaking energy of a local area.

Natural maintainability has turned into an undeniably vital thought in contemporary structural decisions. Green structure advancements, environmentally friendly power frameworks, and feasible materials are vital parts of engineering plans that expect to orchestrate with natural standards. The idea of biophilic plan, which integrates normal components into fabricated conditions, upgrades the visual allure of spaces as well as encourages a feeling of association with nature. Building decisions that focus on energy effectiveness, squander decrease, and biological responsiveness add to the general congruity between human-made structures and the common habitat.

On the other hand, the disregard of reasonable practices can bring about disharmony with the climate. The biological effect of structures, from asset concentrated development materials to energy-consuming frameworks, has incited a reconsideration of design decisions. The unreasonable utilization of non-sustainable assets, the absence of thought for energy-effective plans, and the dismissal for green structure practices can prompt a discordant connection between human-made structures and the regular environments they possess.

In the domain of private engineering, the decisions in home plan straightforwardly affect the tenants' prosperity and personal satisfaction. The standards of feng shui, an old Chinese practice that looks to orchestrate people with their environmental elements, feature the significance of design decisions in making agreeable living spaces. The plan of rooms, the direction of entryways and windows, and the utilization of regular components all assume a part in encouraging positive energy stream and equilibrium inside a home. Engineering decisions that line up with feng shui standards intend to establish homegrown conditions that help wellbeing.

The idea of engineering congruity is a multi-layered investigation that stretches out past the simple plan of structures and designs. It exemplifies the consistent joining of structure, capability, social setting, and style to make a bound together and cognizant setting. Whether in verifiable milestones, contemporary metropolitan scenes, or fictitious universes, the effect of design decisions on the general concordance of a setting is significant, impacting the manner in which individuals connect with their surroundings, forming social characters, and, surprisingly, adding to more extensive cultural stories.

Authentic landmarks frequently act as ageless instances of structural agreement. Think about the lofty pyramids of Giza in Egypt, developed around 2560 BCE. These huge designs, principally the Incomparable Pyramid of Khufu, are wonders of designing as well as impressions of the social and strict convictions of old Egyptians. The arrangement of the pyramids with heavenly bodies, the accuracy in development, and the unpredictable entombment chambers inside manifest a congruity that rises above the actual domain. These compositional decisions were directed by useful contemplations as well as by a profound association with enormous standards and a longing to make enduring landmarks that fit with the vast request.

Essentially, the traditional design of old Greece, exemplified by the Parthenon on the Acropolis in Athens, mirrors a promise to adjust, extent, and stylish solidarity. The

Doric sections, entablature, and pediments of the Parthenon encapsulate a feeling of visual balance. The building decisions made by Iktinos and Phidias were not only utilitarian yet tried to fit with the philosophical goals of antiquated Greece, commending the collaboration between magnificence, reason, and social personality.

Pushing ahead so as to the Renaissance, the building choices made in the update of Rome by Pope Sixtus V and his metropolitan organizer Georges-Eugène Haussmann in sixteenth century Paris show the way that cautious arranging can add to the general concordance of a city. The production of terrific streets, uniform structure veneers, and stupendous squares changed tumultuous archaic metropolitan scenes into organized, tastefully satisfying cityscapes. The conscious decisions in metropolitan arranging addressed functional worries as well as added to a visual cognizance that formed the character of both Rome and Paris, making an agreeable metropolitan encounter.

On the other hand, endless suburbia in the contemporary period addresses a takeoff from these standards, with its low-thickness improvement, divided areas, and accentuation on auto driven plan. Such decisions can prompt an absence of visual union, decreased openness, and a reduced feeling of local area. The rambling idea of urban areas that focus on individualized versatility and rural extension frequently disturbs the general concordance of the metropolitan setting, adding to ecological debasement and social detachment.

Social character assumes a critical part in the effect of engineering decisions on congruity. The Taj Mahal in Agra, India, remains as a demonstration of the blend of different social impacts. Authorized by Ruler Shah Jahan in the seventeenth 100 years, the Taj Mahal mixes Persian, Ottoman, and Indian building styles. The white marble structure, decorated with mind boggling flower themes and calligraphy, mirrors the Mughal obligation to greatness and the agreeable combination of social variety. structural decisions in the plan of the Taj Mahal praise the Mughal social way of life as well as reverberate with an all inclusive feeling of magnificence and otherworldliness.

Conversely, examples where structural decisions conflict with social setting can bring about disharmony. The burden of Western design styles in non-Western settings during times of colonization frequently prompted visual cacophony. The juxtaposition of neoclassical European structures in locales of Africa, Asia, or the Americas disturbed the social texture, making a discordant connection between the fabricated climate and the native setting. Such design decisions were much of the time established in frontier aspirations, reflecting power elements and social uneven characters.

Inspecting the effect of compositional decisions on congruity requires a granular investigation of individual structures and their commitment to the visual and experiential lucidness of a cityscape. In Paris, the compositional decisions made during the mid-nineteenth hundred years, directed by Noble Haussmann's vision, changed the cityscape into a model of metropolitan congruity. The terrific avenues, uniform veneers, and the consolidation of public spaces improved the tasteful solidarity of the city. The conscious arranging choices addressed reasonable contemplations as well as added to a visual rationality that characterizes the personality of Paris right up to the present day.

Nonetheless, contemporary metropolitan conditions frequently wrestle with the test of keeping up with visual congruity when independence overshadows context oriented mix. The expansion of high rises in certain cityscapes, driven by a longing for notable milestones and business practicality, can prompt an absence of visual union. The juxtaposition of dissimilar structural styles and scales might bring about a horizon that comes up short on agreeable stream and progression found in urban communities with more controlled and logically touchy preparation. The quest for singularity in structural articulation can accidentally upset the general amicability of the metropolitan climate, decreasing the visual lucidness and social personality of the city.

Fictitious universes give an exceptional material to investigate the deliberate disturbance or improvement of congruity through building decisions. J.K. Rowling's portrayal of Hogwarts School of Black magic and Wizardry in the Harry Potter series represents how design choices add to the general concordance of a made up setting. The different building styles, charmed highlights, and mysterious components of Hogwarts line up with the fantastical idea of the story, making a setting that resounds with a feeling of marvel and union. purposeful decisions in the plan of Hogwarts add to the vivid experience of the made up world, upgrading the general agreement of the story.

On the other hand, the purposeful disharmony in structural decisions can be utilized to convey explicit account subjects. In tragic settings, for example, the cutting edge cityscapes portrayed in films like "Edge Sprinter," the design decisions stress cacophony, rot, and a feeling of severe futurism. The transcending megastructures, rambling neon-lit streetscapes, and juxtaposition of old and new design components make an air of friction. This deliberate interruption of building concordance fills in as a visual illustration for the tragic stories, reflecting cultural rot, mechanical overabundance, and the outcomes of unrestrained urbanization.

In reality, the effect of engineering decisions on congruity is especially obvious in the plan of public spaces. Placemaking, an idea that underscores the formation of conditions cultivating social cooperation and a feeling of local area, depends intensely on smart building decisions. Public squares like Piazza San Marco in Venice or Court City hall leader in Madrid represent how building choices add to the general congruity of a space. The selection of materials, the plan of seating, the reconciliation of vegetation, and the presence of design milestones all assume a part in molding the environment and usefulness of these public spaces.

On the other hand, ineffectively planned public spaces can prompt disharmony and an absence of metro commitment. Spaces that focus on vehicular traffic over common agreeable plan or need welcoming components like seating, lighting, and public workmanship might beat local area collaboration down. The building decisions made in the plan of public spaces impact the social elements, inclusivity, and by and large energy of a local area.

Natural maintainability has turned into an undeniably pivotal thought in contemporary structural decisions. Green structure advances, environmentally friendly power frameworks, and manageable materials are indispensable parts of compositional plans that intend to fit with biological standards. The idea of biophilic plan, which integrates normal components into constructed conditions, upgrades the visual allure of spaces as well as encourages a feeling of association with nature. Compositional decisions that focus on energy effectiveness, squander decrease, and biological responsiveness add to the general agreement between human-made structures and the regular habitat.

On the other hand, the disregard of reasonable practices can bring about disharmony with the climate. The environmental effect of structures, from asset concentrated development materials to energy-consuming frameworks, has provoked a reconsideration of engineering decisions. The inordinate utilization of non-inexhaustible assets, the absence of thought for energy-effective plans, and the dismissal for green structure practices can prompt a discordant connection between human-made structures and the normal environments they occupy.

In the domain of private engineering, the decisions in home plan straightforwardly affect the tenants' prosperity and personal satisfaction. The standards of feng shui, an old Chinese practice that looks to fit people with their environmental elements, feature the significance of engineering decisions in making agreeable living spaces. The game plan of rooms, the direction of entryways and windows, and the utilization of normal components all assume a part in encouraging positive energy stream and equilibrium inside a home. Compositional decisions that line up with feng shui standards expect to establish homegrown conditions that help wellbeing, success, and by and large amicability for the tenants.

On the other hand, homes that need thought for essential standards of usefulness, ergonomics, and style might bring about discordant day to day environments. Inadequately planned spaces that obstruct normal light, frustrate ventilation, or need appropriate protection can adversely affect the physical and mental prosperity of occupants. decisions in the plan and design of private spaces add to the general amicability of people's regular routines, impacting their solace, usefulness, and feeling of association with their environmental elements.

All in all, the effect of building decisions on the general concordance of a setting is a nuanced and complex thought. From verifiable landmarks that typify social goals to contemporary cityscapes that reflect metropolitan arranging ways of thinking, and from fictitious universes that transport crowds to creative domains to private spaces that shape the day to day routines of people, design winds around a mind boggling embroidery of visual, social, and experiential components.

Whether adding to a feeling of request, equilibrium, and solidarity, or purposefully upsetting assumptions for story or emblematic purposes, structural decisions stay a strong power in molding the human experience and the conditions we occupy.

As social orders wrestle with the difficulties of urbanization, social variety, and natural maintainability, the job of smart and deliberate structural decisions turns out to be progressively vital as one inside the constructed climate and the more extensive social texture. The convergence of usefulness, feel, social responsiveness, and environmental obligation gives designers and metropolitan organizers a powerful material whereupon to create spaces that reverberate with a feeling of solidarity, intelligence, and persevering through magnificence. Through a cautious thought of verifiable points of reference, contemporary developments, and future-situated plan standards, the mission for compositional congruity keeps on molding the manner in which we see, possess, and collaborate with the spaces we call home.

Chapter 7

Societal Harmony and Conflict

In the mind boggling embroidery of human life, the idea of cultural congruity and struggle is woven into the actual texture of our aggregate insight. Society, as a complicated trap of interconnected people, is described by the unique transaction of different components, going from social standards and values to financial designs, political organizations, and relational connections. At the core of this multifaceted dance lies the quest for equilibrium and solidarity, appearing differently in relation to the unavoidable gratings that emerge from contending interests and varying perspectives.

Cultural concordance, an optimistic vision that has energized the desires of developments over the entire course of time, typifies the idea of a quiet concurrence among people and gatherings. It suggests a condition of balance where various parts of society capability in show, encouraging common getting it, collaboration, and shared thriving. Accomplishing such congruity requests the fragile organization of different elements, including civil rights, impartial circulation of assets, and the development of an aggregate ethos that focuses on solidarity over division.

At its center, cultural agreement is profoundly interwoven with the idea of civil rights. The quest for equity is a consistently developing excursion that looks to address authentic imbalances, separation, and foundational predispositions implanted in the texture of social orders. Chasing after cultural congruity, it becomes basic to destroy boundaries that prevent the full and equivalent investment, everything being equal, no matter what their experience, personality, or financial status. A general public that maintains the standards of civil rights endeavors to establish a climate where each individual has the potential chance to flourish and add to the aggregate prosperity.

Monetary designs assume a critical part in molding the elements of cultural congruity. In an ideal situation, financial frameworks would be intended to guarantee fair dissemination of riches, limiting the distinct variations that frequently lead to social distress. Nonetheless, the fact of the matter is many times described by a mind boggling interchange of force elements, where monetary imbalance turns into a wellspring of strain and struggle. The quest for cultural concordance requires a basic assessment of financial models, with an emphasis on making frameworks that focus on the benefit of everyone, supportability, and inclusivity.

Political establishments, as the overseeing systems of society, use huge impact in either encouraging concordance or sustaining struggle. An equitable and straightforward political framework fills in as a foundation for cultural prosperity, guaranteeing portrayal, responsibility, and the security of principal privileges. In actuality, defilement, dictatorship, and the disintegration of popularity based values can raise friction and subvert the actual underpinnings of cultural concordance. Finding some kind of harmony among power and individual opportunities is fundamental to explore the intricacies of administration and develop a general public that values equity and solidarity.

Social variety, while improving the woven artwork of society, likewise presents difficulties to the accomplishment of congruity. Social standards and values, when embraced and praised, add to an energetic social embroidery. Be that as it may, when contrasts lead to rejection, segregation, or the burden of one social point of view over others, it turns into a wellspring of contention. Building cultural amicability requires an appreciation for variety, combined with endeavors to connect social partitions through discourse, schooling, and the advancement of social trade.

Relational connections, the structure blocks of cultural communications, assume a pivotal part in forming the general congruity of a local area. The nature of human associations, established in sympathy, regard, and grasping, impacts the social texture. Sound connections encourage a feeling of having a place and local area, sustaining a climate where people feel upheld and esteemed. Then again, cracked connections set apart by doubt, hostility, and bias can lead to cultural strife. The development of relational abilities and the advancement of a culture of sympathy are essential to encouraging the concordance that ties people together.

In any case, the quest for cultural congruity isn't without its difficulties, and clashes frequently arise as a characteristic outcome of different interests, values, and points of view. The wellsprings of contention are diverse, going from financial variations and political fights for control to social conflicts and personality based pressures. Understanding the underlying drivers of contention is significant to concocting compelling techniques for goal and counteraction.

Monetary differences, exacerbated by inconsistent admittance to assets and valuable open doors, stand as an unavoidable wellspring of cultural clash. The enlarging hole between the well-to-do and the underestimated can raise disdain, social turmoil, and a feeling of bad form. Tending to financial abberations requires far reaching changes that focus on impartial dispersion of assets, fair work practices, and strategies pointed toward inspiring underestimated networks. Without such intercessions, monetary disparity turns into a favorable place for social strains that can grow into additional significant struggles.

Political battles for control and administration disappointments are powerful impetuses for cultural clash. At the point when organizations intended to maintain equity and address the interests of individuals vacillate, trust disintegrates, and discontent putrefies. Tyrant systems, defilement, and the disintegration of popularity based values can light friendly developments and fights as people try to recover their organization and request responsibility. Settling political struggles involves tending to prompt complaints as well as building vigorous establishments that maintain majority rule standards and defend the privileges, everything being equal.

Social conflicts, frequently filled by ethnocentrism and the attestation of one social authority over others, add to social disunity. In a globalized world, where different societies converge and entwine, exploring social contrasts requires a nuanced approach that values pluralism and shared regard. Instruction, intercultural discourse, and the advancement of social trade can act as components to connect partitions and cultivate a feeling of shared humankind. Inability to address social pressures might prompt the entrenchment of personality based clashes, blocking the acknowledgment of cultural concordance.

Character based strains, whether established in race, religion, orientation, or different markers of personality, address an unavoidable test to cultural congruity. Bias, separation, and rejection in light of character can break networks and fuel enmity. Beating character based clashes requires a guarantee to variety, consideration, and the destroying of biased rehearses. Training and mindfulness building drives assume a urgent part in testing imbued predispositions and encouraging a feeling of normal mankind that rises above individual contrasts.

Ecological corruption, driven by unreasonable practices and the double-dealing of regular assets, represents a danger to cultural congruity. The consumption of biological systems, environmental change, and ecological fiascos can fuel existing social imbalances and trigger contentions over scant assets.

Building an agreeable society requires a pledge to ecological manageability, mindful asset the board, and aggregate endeavors to address the difficulties presented by environmental change. Inability to focus on natural stewardship might prompt struggles over lessening assets, further stressing the sensitive equilibrium of cultural agreement.

The job of innovation in forming cultural elements is a two sided deal, equipped for both cultivating concordance and filling struggle. On one hand, innovative headways offer extraordinary open doors for correspondence, joint effort, and the scattering of data. Then again, the abuse of innovation, like the spread of falsehood, digital fighting, and the disintegration of security, can sabotage cultural attachment. Finding some kind of harmony between tackling the advantages of innovation and relieving its potential damages is fundamental for building an amicable society in the computerized age.

In exploring the intricacies of cultural congruity and struggle, the job of training arises as a key part. Schooling fills in as an incredible asset for molding perspectives, cultivating decisive reasoning, and imparting values that advance collaboration and understanding. An all encompassing school system that tends to scholastic subjects as well as friendly and close to home learning is instrumental in developing the abilities and viewpoints required for exploring the complexities of a different and interconnected world. By advancing sympathy, social mindfulness, and a feeling of shared liability, schooling turns into an impetus for cultural congruity.

Endeavors to fabricate and support cultural congruity require a complex methodology that traverses individual, local area, and institutional levels. At the singular level, encouraging sympathy, receptiveness, and a guarantee to civil rights lays the basis for agreeable connections. Local area level drives, for example, grassroots developments, social trade programs, and cooperative activities, add to the production of comprehensive and strong social orders. Institutional changes, incorporating political, financial, and social circles, are fundamental for resolving foundational issues that upset congruity and sustain struggle.

Compromise components assume a critical part in overseeing and moderating cultural pressures when they emerge. Peacebuilding drives, intervention cycles, and exchange stages offer roads for tending to complaints, encouraging compromise, and building spans between clashing gatherings. Putting resources into compromise limits at nearby, public, and worldwide levels is critical for forestalling the heightening of contentions and advancing manageable harmony.

Worldwide collaboration and tact likewise assume a vital part chasing worldwide cultural concordance. In an interconnected world, where the activities of one country can have broad ramifications, coordinated effort on issues, for example, environmental change, financial disparity, and common freedoms is basic.

Conciliatory endeavors pointed toward encouraging figuring out, exchange, and participation add to the making of a more amicable worldwide local area.

The job of authority in molding cultural elements couldn't possibly be more significant. Visionary and moral authority is instrumental in directing social orders towards amicability by encouraging comprehensive strategies, maintaining majority rule esteems, and tending to the underlying drivers of contention. Pioneers who focus on the benefit of everyone over thin interests, embrace variety, and support equity add to the production of a social structure that values concordance as an aggregate objective.

All in all, the transaction between cultural concordance and struggle is a mind boggling and dynamic peculiarity that characterizes the direction of human social orders. The quest for concordance requires a deliberate work to address the underlying drivers of contention, going from financial differences and political administration to social conflicts and personality based pressures. Schooling, sympathy, and compromise systems act as fundamental devices in building versatile and comprehensive social orders.

Cultural concordance is certainly not a static state however a continuous cycle that requests persistent reflection, variation, and aggregate activity. As we explore the difficulties of the contemporary world, the vision of an agreeable society stays an encouraging sign, motivating people, networks, and countries to pursue a future where solidarity, equity, and understanding win.

7.1 Examine social structures and their impact on the world.

Social designs structure the foundation of human social orders, giving the systems inside which people collaborate, organizations capability, and aggregate characters arise. Inspecting social designs and their effect on the world involves digging into the multifaceted trap of connections, standards, and establishments that shape the elements of human life. From nuclear families to worldwide frameworks, social designs impact how we sort out ourselves, distribute assets, and explore the intricacies of conjunction.

At the central level, family structures assume a crucial part in molding individual characters and cultural qualities. Families act as the essential socialization specialists, sending social standards, values, and customs starting with one age then onto the next. The elements inside families, affected by variables like orientation jobs, social assumptions, and financial status, add to the development of individual perspectives and desires. Understanding the complexities of family structures is fundamental for getting a handle on the underlying foundations of cultural qualities and the transmission of social capital starting with one age then onto the next.

Moving past the nuclear family, neighborhood networks address one more layer of social design that altogether influences the world. Local area structures envelop neighborhoods, towns, and towns, encouraging a feeling of having a place and divided personality between occupants.

The strength of local area ties impacts social union, aggregate critical thinking, and the general prosperity of people. The elements of neighborhood networks shape the social texture, deciding the degree to which people feel associated with each other and participated in the more extensive cultural setting.

In the more extensive setting of cultural association, organizations arise as basic parts of social designs. Instructive foundations, government bodies, financial frameworks, and strict associations on the whole add to the arrangement and guideline of cultural standards. Instructive foundations, for example, assume a crucial part in molding the qualities, abilities, and points of view of people, impacting their jobs in the more extensive social design. Government organizations, then again, lay out the lawful and political structure inside which social orders work, forming power elements, equity frameworks, and the conveyance of assets.

Monetary designs, one more foundation of social association, apply a significant impact on worldwide elements. Entrepreneur, communist, and blended financial frameworks each bring particular benefits and difficulties, affecting abundance circulation, admittance to assets, and generally speaking cultural prosperity. Financial designs add to the propagation or easing of disparities inside and among countries, influencing everything from individual open doors to international connections. Analyzing monetary designs is urgent for figuring out the more extensive ramifications of abundance gathering, asset designation, and the interconnectedness of worldwide economies.

The domain of legislative issues further highlights the effect of social designs on the world. Political designs, whether popularity based, dictator, or mixture, decide the dispersion of force, portrayal, and dynamic cycles inside a general public. The association of political frameworks impacts the assurance of common liberties, law and order, and the responsibility of pioneers to their constituents. The assessment of political designs uncovers how administration shapes the direction of countries, the idea of worldwide relations, and the quest for equity on a worldwide scale.

Social designs, profoundly implanted in the texture of social orders, add to the extravagance and variety of human experience. Language, customs, convictions, and imaginative articulations structure the embroidery of social designs, molding individual personalities and shared mindset. Social designs impact how social orders see themselves as well as other people, encouraging a feeling of shared legacy or, on occasion, adding to ethnocentrism and social contentions. Understanding the complexities of social designs is fundamental for exploring the intricacies of a globalized world, where various societies converge and interface.

Orientation structures, a subset of social association, assume an essential part in molding power elements, assumptions, and valuable open doors inside social orders. Orientation jobs and standards impact how people explore their own and proficient lives, influencing all that from profession decisions to relational peculiarities.

Inspecting orientation structures discloses the fundamental difficulties of orientation disparity, segregation, and the continuous battle for orientation value. The effect of orientation structures reaches out past individual encounters, molding cultural perspectives, strategies, and the dissemination of assets.

Social separation, an unavoidable part of social designs, appears through the division of social orders into various classes, positions, or gatherings. Financial, instructive, and word related inconsistencies add to social definition, making orders that influence people's admittance to amazing open doors and assets. Analyzing social delineation divulges the fundamental disparities implanted in friendly designs, featuring the crossing points of race, class, orientation, and other personality markers. Social delineation is a focal point through which to break down the circulation of honor and the obstructions that upset social portability.

Globalization, an overall power in the contemporary world, has changed the scene of social designs. The interconnectedness of economies, correspondence frameworks, and societies has obscured customary limits, reshaping how social orders associate and impact each other. The assessment of worldwide social designs uncovers the many-sided organizations of exchange, data trade, and social dissemination that portray the advanced period. Worldwide designs, including worldwide associations, settlements, and partnerships, assume a focal part in tending to worldwide difficulties, for example, environmental change, pandemics, and basic freedoms infringement.

The effect of social designs on the world reaches out to ecological elements, as human social orders communicate with and impact the regular world. The association of social orders, monetary exercises, and utilization designs add to ecological corruption, environmental change, and the exhaustion of regular assets. Analyzing the natural effect of social designs highlights the earnest requirement for maintainable practices, protection endeavors, and aggregate liability in tending to biological difficulties.

Mechanical designs, a characterizing component of the contemporary time, have reshaped the manner in which social orders capability and collaborate. Data and correspondence advances, man-made brainpower, and computerized stages have changed correspondence, business, and admittance to data. Inspecting mechanical designs uncovers both the amazing open doors and difficulties presented by fast innovative headways, including issues connected with protection, network safety, and the advanced gap. The joining of innovation into social designs requires cautious thought of its moral ramifications and the potential for molding the future direction of social orders.

Social developments, arising in light of seen treacheries or fundamental issues, mirror the dynamism of social designs. Developments pushing for social equality, natural equity, orientation correspondence, and different causes challenge existing designs and request cultural change.

The assessment of social developments gives experiences into the flexibility of human organization, the potential for aggregate activity, and the job of grassroots drives in reshaping social designs.

Looking at social designs and their effect on the world requires a nuanced comprehension of force elements, foundational disparities, and the transaction of different variables that shape human social orders. It requires recognizing both the positive commitments and the innate defects inside friendly designs, perceiving that they are not static however dependent upon development and change. Social designs, as mind boggling and multi-layered as they might be, are the framework whereupon the accounts of mankind's set of experiences, progress, and difficulties unfurl.

7.2 Discuss how conflicts and resolutions contribute to the overall harmony.

Clashes, intrinsic in the human experience, act as pots of progress, testing the versatility of people and social orders the same. Inseparably connected to the quest for congruity, clashes and their goals assume essential parts in molding the elements of human cooperations, affecting social designs, and adding to the general woven artwork of aggregate presence.

Struggle, extensively characterized as a conflict of interests, values, or points of view, is a ubiquitous power in both individual connections and cultural designs. At the singular level, clashes might emerge from contrasting convictions, wants, or objectives, while for a bigger scope, cultural contentions might appear as political battles, social conflicts, or monetary inconsistencies. The certainty of contention is established in the variety of human encounters, where fluctuating viewpoints and interests coincide.

Inside the domain of individual connections, clashes can be seen as any open doors for development and understanding. Conflicts, when drawn closer with receptiveness and an eagerness to participate in productive exchange, give a pathway to people to verbalize their requirements, express their viewpoints, and cultivate common comprehension. In this specific situation, goals become the scaffolds that range the holes made by clashes, prompting reinforced connections and more profound associations.

In addition, clashes inside private connections act as mirrors mirroring the intricacies of human feelings and relational elements. The goal of such struggles requires compassion, powerful correspondence, and split the difference. As people explore the complexities of clashing cravings or viewpoints, the course of goal turns into an extraordinary excursion, encouraging capacity to understand individuals on a deeper level and fortifying the obligations of trust.

On a cultural level, clashes frequently rise up out of foundational issues imbued in friendly designs. Monetary differences, political battles for control, social conflicts, and character based pressures address wellsprings of contention that request consideration and goal.

The goal of cultural struggles is instrumental chasing cultural concordance, as it tends to main drivers, advances equity, and lays the basis for a more evenhanded and comprehensive social request.

Monetary struggles, coming from differences in riches and admittance to assets, can prompt social turmoil and discontent. The goal of financial struggles requires approaches and drives that address disparity, advance fair work rehearses, and guarantee the evenhanded dissemination of assets. In doing as such, social orders draw nearer to a condition of concordance where monetary open doors are open to all, diminishing the potential for social difficulty.

Political contentions, frequently portrayed by fights for control, administration disappointments, or disagreements about values, have significant ramifications for cultural amicability. The goal of political contentions requires the foundation of straightforward and responsible political situation, the insurance of common liberties, and instruments for comprehensive portrayal. A general public that effectively addresses political contentions is one where people trust their foundations, and law and order wins, adding to an agreeable social and world of politics.

Social struggles emerge from dissimilar standards, values, and perspectives inside a general public. These struggles might be established in verifiable complaints, philosophical contrasts, or the attestation of one social character over others. The goal of social struggles includes cultivating social grasping, advancing exchange, and praising variety. Cultural concordance, in this specific circumstance, is accomplished through the acknowledgment and acknowledgment of different social articulations, prompting a more comprehensive and open minded social texture.

Character based clashes, whether revolved around race, religion, orientation, or different markers of personality, present critical difficulties to cultural congruity. The goal of character based clashes requires a pledge to destroying prejudicial works on, testing predispositions, and encouraging inclusivity. Social orders that explore character based clashes effectively perceive the pride and equivalent privileges of each and every person, establishing an agreeable climate where variety isn't just recognized yet celebrated.

Ecological struggles, driven by issues, for example, environmental change, asset consumption, and living space obliteration, address a developing worldwide test. The goal of ecological contentions requires aggregate endeavors to address maintainability, relieve the effect of human exercises in the world, and advance capable stewardship of normal assets. Cultural amicability, in this unique circumstance, is entwined with biological equilibrium, as the prosperity of human social orders is complicatedly associated with the soundness of the climate.

Clashes likewise assume a focal part in forming the course of history through friendly developments. Developments upholding for social liberties, ecological equity, orientation balance, and different causes arise because of seen shameful acts or fundamental issues. These developments address aggregate endeavors to address clashes and achieve positive change. Goals inside the setting of social developments frequently include strategy changes, changes in popular assessment, and the formation of new normal practices that add to an all the more and fair society.

While clashes are intrinsic in the human experience, their goal isn't direct all the time. Successful compromise requires a promise to exchange, compassion, and a common vision of an amicable future. At times, clashes might prompt groundbreaking change, testing existing standards and designs and making ready for an all the more and comprehensive society.

The course of compromise isn't without its difficulties, and it frequently includes wrestling with well established issues and fundamental shameful acts. It requires a readiness to face awkward insights, recognize verifiable wrongs, and work towards fundamental changes that address the main drivers of contentions. Genuine goal goes past simple submission; it looks to make an establishment for enduring concordance by encouraging figuring out, destroying disparities, and building spans among people and networks.

In addition, the job of schooling in compromise couldn't possibly be more significant. Instruction fills in as an integral asset for testing generalizations, cultivating decisive reasoning, and advancing a culture of sympathy. By integrating compromise abilities into instructive educational plans, social orders can outfit people with the apparatuses expected to explore conflicts, span isolates, and add to the general congruity of the local area.

In the worldwide field, clashes between countries have significant ramifications for worldwide amicability. Discretion, discourse, and worldwide collaboration become fundamental apparatuses in settling clashes and cultivating tranquil relations between nations. Worldwide contentions, whether emerging from regional questions, monetary competitions, or philosophical contrasts, require conciliatory endeavors pointed toward figuring out some shared interest, advancing comprehension, and forestalling the heightening of pressures.

Clashes likewise highlight the significance of encouraging a culture of harmony. Building such a culture includes advancing qualities like resilience, participation, and peacefulness. It requires tending to the underlying drivers of contentions and putting resources into drives that add to civil rights, fairness, and the prosperity, everything being equal. A culture of harmony goes past the shortfall of brutality; it epitomizes a promise to making conditions that support concordance, understanding, and shared regard.

In the domain of relational connections, clashes can act as impetuses for self-awareness and self-disclosure. When drawn closer with a mentality of goal instead of evasion, clashes offer people the valuable chance to foster relational abilities, the capacity to understand individuals on a deeper level, and flexibility. The capacity to explore clashes in a valuable way adds to the general prosperity of people and upgrades the nature of connections.

At the cultural level, clashes and their goals add to the development of social designs. Effective peaceful settlements frequently lead to fundamental changes, strategy changes, and changes in cultural perspectives. For instance, verifiable battles for social equality have brought about regulative changes, lawful securities, and a more extensive cultural acknowledgment of the requirement for balance. Likewise, developments pushing for ecological protection have impacted strategies, molded public talk, and added to a developing consciousness of the significance of supportability.

The idea of temporary equity embodies how compromises can add to cultural congruity. In the repercussions of contentions or times of shamefulness, momentary equity looks to address denials of basic liberties, advance responsibility, and make ready for compromise. Instruments, for example, truth and compromise commissions plan to mend cultural injuries by recognizing past wrongs, giving a stage to casualties to share their encounters, and outlining a way towards an additional equitable and amicable future.

On a mental level, the goal of contentions can significantly affect individual prosperity. Unsettled clashes might prompt pressure, nervousness, and stressed connections, while effective compromise can achieve a positive feeling, conclusion, and close to home recuperating. In this sense, the individual component of compromise adds to a more agreeable and adjusted condition of being for people.

7.3 Explore the role of societal dynamics in shaping the setting.

Cultural elements, the complex transaction of different components inside a local area, apply a significant impact on molding the setting wherein people live, connect, and develop. The setting, incorporating physical, social, financial, and political aspects, is definitely not a static scenery however a unique material continually molded and reshaped by the powers of cultural elements. This investigation digs into the multilayered manners by which cultural elements form and characterize the setting, making the background against which human encounters unfurl.

At the core of cultural elements lies the idea of local area, a nexus of connections, standards, and shared values that lead to an aggregate personality. The idea of local area elements altogether influences the setting, deciding the degree of social union, inclusivity, and generally speaking prosperity. In affectionate networks, where relational associations are solid, the setting frequently mirrors a feeling of commonality, trust, and shared liability. Interestingly, divided or partitioned networks might observer a setting set apart by pressure, doubt, and the propagation of social variations.

Social elements, profoundly implanted inside cultural structures, assume a urgent part in forming the setting. Culture includes the convictions, customs, customs, and creative articulations that characterize a local area's personality. The setting turns into an impression of social qualities, with building styles, language decisions, and creative indications reflecting the social subtleties of the general public. Social elements add to the extravagance of the setting, making an embroidery of variety or, at times, leading to social conflicts that impact the physical and social scene.

Monetary elements, one more key aspect of cultural impact, make a permanent imprint on the setting. Financial designs decide asset portion, admittance to open doors, and the general thriving of a local area. In settings where financial differences are predominant, the scene might be portrayed by apparent markers of imbalance — variations in framework, lodging, and public administrations. Going against the norm, in settings where monetary value is really important, the scene might show a more adjusted dispersion of assets, adding to a feeling of social congruity.

Political elements, dug in the administration designs of a general public, use critical impact over the setting. The idea of political frameworks — whether popularity based, tyrant, or cross breed — influences the conveyance of force, dynamic cycles, and the general solidness of the setting. In fairly represented settings, there might be a noticeable accentuation on urban commitment, straightforward administration, and the security of individual privileges, forming the setting to reflect standards of equity and participatory direction. On the other hand, in settings set apart by dictator rule or political flimsiness, the scene might bear the scars of battles for control, limited opportunities, and an absence of political steadiness.

The metropolitan rustic dynamic further complements the job of cultural elements in forming the setting. Metropolitan settings, portrayed by thick populaces, various monetary exercises, and social center points, frequently encapsulate the speedy idea of current cultures. The metropolitan setting reflects cultural yearnings for financial open doors, social trade, and admittance to conveniences. On the other hand, country settings, with their emphasis on farming, affectionate networks, and an association with nature, exemplify an alternate feature of cultural elements, stressing straightforwardness, public ties, and a particular relationship with the climate.

Social separation, an inescapable part of cultural elements, leaves an engraving on the setting by making unmistakable layers inside networks. Separation in light of elements like abundance, schooling, and societal position appears in apparent ways, impacting the physical and social scene. Settings described by articulated social separation may feature selective areas, variations in instructive foundation, and restricted admittance to fundamental administrations, mirroring the inconsistent circulation of assets inside the local area.

Mechanical elements, a characterizing component of contemporary social orders, acquaint another layer with the setting. The reception and combination of innovation shape the actual climate and social communications. Settings with cutting edge innovative frameworks might show a quick moving, interconnected nature, with computerized interfaces, shrewd foundation, and a dependence on virtual correspondence. Then again, settings with restricted admittance to innovation might mirror a more customary or more slow paced lifestyle, underlining up close and personal communications and a dependence on simple frameworks.

Segment elements, impacted by variables like populace development, movement, and age conveyance, add to the setting's organization and character. Developing populaces might prompt metropolitan extension, expanded interest for assets, and changes in land use. Alternately, termination or a maturing segment might bring about contracting networks, changed social elements, and reusing of foundation. The setting turns into a material on which segment shifts work out, impacting the essentialness and strength of the local area.

Ecological elements, firmly entwined with cultural elements, shape the setting through human associations with the normal world. The double-dealing of normal assets, land use practices, and reactions to ecological difficulties add to the actual appearance of the setting. Settings set apart by supportable practices, preservation endeavors, and an agreeable relationship with the climate might mirror a promise to natural equilibrium. On the other hand, settings wrestling with ecological corruption might display indications of contamination, deforestation, and a stressed relationship with the regular environmental elements.

The job of cultural elements in forming the setting isn't bound to the actual scene alone; it reaches out to the immaterial parts of human experience. Accepted practices and values, results of cultural elements, penetrate the setting, affecting way of behaving, assumptions, and the general ethos of the local area. A setting formed by moderate normal practices might focus on inclusivity, variety, and civil rights. On the other hand, a setting secured in moderate qualities might show a more customary or unbending social design.

Cultural elements likewise assume a vital part in emergency and recuperation situations, leaving an enduring effect on the setting. Cataclysmic events, pandemics, or financial slumps can reshape the physical and social scene, prompting changes in framework, relocation examples, and local area flexibility. The recuperation cycle turns into a demonstration of the flexibility and union of the local area, impacting the direction of the setting in the fallout of emergencies.

Local area commitment, a sign of cultural elements, turns into a main thrust in forming the setting. Dynamic cooperation, joint effort, and shared liability add to a lively and responsive local area setting. In settings where local area commitment is cultivated, there might be noticeable indications of aggregate drives, public spaces that energize connection, and a feeling of responsibility and pride among occupants.

On the other hand, settings where local area commitment is restricted may display indications of disengagement, disregard of public spaces, and an absence of shared personality.

With regards to globalization, cultural elements stretch out past neighborhood settings to influence worldwide collaborations. The interconnectedness of social orders, worked with by correspondence innovations and monetary interdependencies, brings about a common worldwide setting. Social trades, monetary patterns, and cooperative endeavors to address worldwide difficulties add to a defining that rises above geological limits, mirroring the aggregate effect of cultural elements on a worldwide scale.

Looking at the job of cultural elements in forming the setting highlights the mind boggling connection between human networks and their surroundings. The setting turns into an impression of cultural qualities, desires, and difficulties, reflecting the perplexing exchange of social, financial, political, and ecological powers. As social orders explore the developing scene of the contemporary world, a comprehension of cultural elements becomes fundamental for imagining and developing settings that advance concordance, flexibility, and a common feeling of prosperity.

The setting of human life is a unique material, formed and shaped by a horde of interconnected powers that on the whole structure the perplexing snare of cultural elements. This investigation dives into the diverse manners by which these cultural elements impact and characterize the settings wherein people live, molding the actual climate as well as the social, monetary, political, and social texture that comprises the scenery of human encounters.

At its center, cultural elements spin around the idea of local area, where connections, standards, and shared values lead to an aggregate personality. This aggregate personality, thusly, makes a permanent imprint on the setting, deciding the degree of social attachment, inclusivity, and generally speaking prosperity. The idea of local area elements altogether impacts the setting, whether it be described areas of strength for by associations, trust, and shared liability in affectionate networks, or pressure, doubt, and social variations in additional divided or isolated ones.

Social elements, profoundly implanted inside cultural systems, assume an essential part in molding the setting. Culture includes the convictions, customs, customs, and creative articulations that characterize a local area's personality. Thus, the setting turns into an impression of these social qualities. Design styles, language decisions, and imaginative signs reflect the social subtleties of the general public, making an unmistakable feeling that adds to the lavishness and variety of the setting. In any case, social elements are not generally agreeable, and conflicts might emerge, affecting the physical and social scene.

Monetary elements, one more pivotal aspect of cultural impact, make a permanent imprint on the setting by deciding asset assignment, admittance to open doors, and in general success. Financial designs direct the dispersion of riches, forming the scene in light of the predominant monetary variations. Settings set apart by articulated monetary imbalances might display noticeable markers like abberations in foundation, lodging, and public administrations, mirroring the inconsistent dissemination of assets inside the local area. On the other hand, settings where financial value is fundamentally important may show a more adjusted circulation, adding to a feeling of social concordance.

Political elements, settled in administration structures, employ critical impact over the setting by deciding the circulation of force, dynamic cycles, and generally speaking strength. The idea of political frameworks, whether majority rule, dictator, or cross breed, influences the scene. Fairly represented settings might underline municipal commitment, straightforward administration, and the insurance of individual freedoms, forming the setting to reflect standards of equity and participatory independent direction. On the other hand, settings set apart by dictator rule or political precariousness might show scars of fights for control, limited opportunities, and an absence of political steadiness.

The metropolitan provincial dynamic emphasizes the job of cultural elements in molding the setting. Metropolitan settings, portrayed by thick populaces, various financial exercises, and social center points, frequently exemplify the high speed nature of present day cultures. The setting in metropolitan regions reflects cultural desires for financial open doors, social trade, and admittance to conveniences. Going against the norm, country settings, with their emphasis on farming, affectionate networks, and an association with nature, exemplify an alternate feature of cultural elements, underscoring straightforwardness, common ties, and a particular relationship with the climate.

Social delineation, an unavoidable part of cultural elements, leaves an engraving on the setting by making unmistakable layers inside networks. Settings portrayed by articulated social separation may exhibit select areas, abberations in instructive framework, and restricted admittance to fundamental administrations. These appearances mirror the disparities imbued in the social construction, affecting the physical and social scene.

Innovative elements, a characterizing component of contemporary social orders, acquaint another layer with the setting. The reception and coordination of innovation shape the actual climate and social associations. In settings with cutting edge mechanical foundations, the scene might display a speedy, interconnected nature with computerized interfaces, brilliant framework, and a dependence on virtual correspondence. On the other hand, settings with restricted admittance to innovation might mirror a more conventional or more slow paced lifestyle, underlining eye to eye cooperations and a dependence on simple frameworks.

Segment elements, affected by variables like populace development, movement, and age dissemination, add to the setting's arrangement and character. Developing populaces might prompt metropolitan extension, expanded interest for assets, and changes in land use. Alternately, eradication or a maturing segment might bring about contracting networks, changed social elements, and reusing of foundation. The setting turns into a material on which segment shifts work out, impacting the essentialness and strength of the local area.

Ecological elements, firmly entwined with cultural elements, shape the setting through human associations with the normal world. The abuse of regular assets, land use practices, and reactions to natural difficulties add to the actual appearance of the setting. Settings set apart by maintainable practices, protection endeavors, and an amicable relationship with the climate might mirror a promise to environmental equilibrium. On the other hand, settings wrestling with ecological debasement might display indications of contamination, deforestation, and a stressed relationship with the regular environmental elements.

The job of cultural elements in forming the setting isn't bound to the actual scene alone; it reaches out to the elusive parts of human experience. Normal practices and values, results of cultural elements, pervade the setting, affecting way of behaving, assumptions, and the general ethos of the local area. A setting molded by moderate normal practices might focus on inclusivity, variety, and civil rights. On the other hand, a setting secured in moderate qualities might display a more conventional or unbending social design.

Cultural elements likewise assume a significant part in emergency and recuperation situations, leaving an enduring effect on the setting. Cataclysmic events, pandemics, or monetary slumps can reshape the physical and social scene, prompting changes in framework, relocation examples, and local area versatility. The recuperation cycle turns into a demonstration of the versatility and union of the local area, impacting the direction of the setting in the consequence of emergencies.

Local area commitment, a sign of cultural elements, turns into a main impetus in molding the setting. Dynamic interest, joint effort, and shared liability add to an energetic and responsive local area setting. In settings where local area commitment is cultivated, there might be noticeable indications of aggregate drives, public spaces that empower communication, and a feeling of responsibility and pride among occupants. On the other hand, settings where local area commitment is restricted may display indications of detachment, disregard of public spaces, and an absence of shared character.

With regards to globalization, cultural elements stretch out past neighborhood settings to influence worldwide communications. The interconnectedness of social orders, worked with by correspondence advancements and financial interdependencies, brings about a common worldwide setting.

Social trades, monetary patterns, and cooperative endeavors to address worldwide difficulties add to a defining that rises above geological limits, mirroring the aggregate effect of cultural elements on a worldwide scale.

Chapter 8

Seasons and Cycles

Seasons and cycles weave the mind boggling embroidery of our reality, a cadenced dance that unfurls across the material of time. Nature, with its steadily evolving shades, reflects the recurrent examples that administer our lives, helping us to remember the unending rhythmic movement that characterizes the human experience.

The world, a living demonstration of the progression of time, goes through a consistent transformation through the four seasons. Spring envoys the resurrection of life, an ensemble of varieties and scents that burst forward from the lethargic earth. The air is loaded up with the sweet song of birdsong, and blossoms spread out their petals in a festival of reestablishment. As the days protract, a feeling of imperativeness saturates the environment, moving an aggregate arousing.

Summer follows with its glow and overflow, a period of development and realization. The sun, a considerate watchman, washes the land in its brilliant hug, persuading harvests to mature and welcoming individuals outside to luxuriate in its brilliant shine. Long days stretch into lazy nights, and the world appears to stop in a sunlit dream, suspended in the immortal excellence existing apart from everything else.

Pre-winter lays out the scene in a rich embroidery of chestnut and gold, flagging a time of reflection and change. The air turns fresh, and passes on vacillate to the ground in an effortless dance, giving up to the certainty of progress. It is a time of collect, an opportunity to assemble the products of work and express gratefulness for the overflow that supports us. As sunlight winds down, the world gets ready for a steady drop into the tranquil reflection of winter.

Winter shows up, hung in a shroud of tranquility and serenity. The world sleeps underneath a sweeping of snow, and the chill in the air energizes reflection and consideration. Trees stand exposed, their branches scratched against the pale sky like complicated lacework. Winter is a time of rest, a vital delay in the never-ending pattern of development and rot. It welcomes us to turn internal, to look for warmth and comfort in the hug of hearth and home.

These four seasons, similar to the parts of an infinite novel, rehash their immortal story many years. However, inside this great embroidery, there are cycles inside cycles, more modest rhythms that reverberation the bigger rhythm of the seasons. The moon, a quiet observer in the night sky, fluctuates in a never-ending hit the dance floor with the tides. Its stages mark the progression of time, directing the tides of the sea and affecting the way of behaving of animals both incredible and little.

The feminine cycle, a remarkably human mood, reflects the lunar dance in its rhythmic movement. Ladies, sensitive to the unobtrusive rhythm of their bodies, experience the changing tides of fruitfulness and period. A cycle traverses the course of a month, a scaled down impression of the bigger examples that oversee the regular world. In regarding this cycle, ladies associate with the basic powers of creation and restoration that course through the actual texture of presence.

Past the divine and natural cycles, there are social and cultural rhythms that shape the human story. The wheel of the year, celebrated in different customs and religions, denotes the defining moments of the seasons with celebrations and ceremonies. These repetitive observances interface networks to the land, the universe, and the immortal customs that have molded human awareness all through the ages.

In farming, the planting and gathering of harvests follow the musicality of the seasons, a hit the dance floor with the earth that supports life. The old act of yield turn mirrors a comprehension of the significance of equilibrium and reestablishment in keeping up with the fruitfulness of the dirt. As people have developed, so too have their strategies for tackling the patterns of nature to guarantee the wealth of the reap.

Economies, as well, follow repeating examples of win and fail. The persistent quest for development and progress is tempered by unavoidable times of downturn and reflection. The financial cycle, with its pinnacles and box, is a demonstration of the interconnectedness of worldwide business sectors and the sensitive equilibrium expected to support success.

Human connections, similar to the evolving seasons, go through their own patterns of development, development, and at times, decline. The underlying flush of fervor and disclosure in another relationship gives way to the more profound, more nuanced tints of friendship and understanding. Similarly as the seasons show us the excellence of fleetingness, connections help us to remember the always moving elements that portray the human experience.

In the great embroidery of time, the ascent and fall of civic establishments follow a repeating design. Realms that once remained as transcending landmarks to human accomplishment in the long run disintegrate, clearing a path for new social orders to arise. The illustrations of history are written in the patterns of force, triumph, and recharging that reverberation across the ages.

Innovation, a main impetus of present day civilization, follows its own fast patterns of development and out of date quality. The tireless speed of innovative headway drives society forward, changing the manner in which we live, work, and communicate.

However, with each jump forward, there is an unavoidable shadow of outdated nature that projects its pall over the once state of the art developments of days of old.

In the midst of these cycles, the normal world fills in as a consistent sign of the sensitive equilibrium that supports life on The planet. The carbon cycle, a crucial interaction that manages the piece of the climate, represents the interconnectedness of every living thing. Plants retain carbon dioxide through photosynthesis, delivering oxygen high up and giving the establishment to the perplexing trap of life.

Likewise, the water cycle, an immortal dance of vanishing, buildup, and precipitation, guarantees the constant flow of water on our planet. Streams stream, seas rhythmic movement, and downpour supports the land, supporting environments and cultivating biodiversity. The fragile harmony of these cycles is a demonstration of the strength and versatility of life in the entirety of its heap structures.

In the tremendous scopes of the universe, heavenly bodies follow their own glorious cycles. The circles of planets around the sun, the dance of worlds in the vast scope, and the existence patterns of stars themselves are spectacular appearances of the repeating idea of the universe. Birth, demise, and resurrection unfurl for a vast scope, helping us to remember our unassuming spot in the fabulous embroidery of presence.

As we explore the patterns of life, both microcosmic and macrocosmic, there arises a significant acknowledgment of the interconnectedness, everything being equal. The seasons, with their musical rhythm, reflect the timeless cycles that administer the universe. From the minute dance of molecules to the divine expressive dance of worlds, the actual universe is a demonstration of the persevering through guideline of repeating reestablishment.

In the dance of seasons and cycles, there is astuteness to be gathered. An insight discusses temporariness, of the certainty of progress, and the magnificence inborn in the patterns of life. Embracing this insight permits us to explore the difficulties and vulnerabilities of presence with beauty and versatility.

The seasons show us the craft of giving up, as fall passes on give up to the breeze, and winter says goodbye to the glow of summer. In the pattern of the moon, there is an example in the back and forth movement of life's tides, an update that change is the main steady. The rural cycles welcome us to develop an amicable relationship with the land, perceiving our job as stewards of the earth.

In the patterns of human connections, there is a chance for development and change. As the times of affection and friendship advance, we figure out how to explore the fragile harmony among freedom and association. The ascent and fall of civic establishments, set apart by the recurrent tides of history, ask us to ponder the temporariness of force and the getting through tradition of human inventiveness.

Innovation, in its steady patterns of development, provokes us to adjust and advance. The fast speed of progress in the cutting edge world welcomes us to embrace an outlook of ceaseless learning and transformation. The financial cycles, with their unavoidable variances, brief us to reevaluate the idea of flourishing and rethink our qualities despite vulnerability.

In the stupendous embroidery of time, the patterns of the regular world allure us to venerate the interconnected snare of life. The carbon cycle and water cycle help us to remember our obligation to secure and save the fragile equilibrium of biological systems. The enormous cycles, with their unbelievable scales, rouse a feeling of stunningness and modesty despite the limitlessness of the universe.

As we explore the seasons and patterns of our individual and aggregate excursions, there is a challenge to adjust ourselves to the basic rhythms that shape our reality. Similarly as a landscaper watches out for the necessities of plants through the evolving seasons, we, as well, can develop care and mindfulness as we cross the scenes of our lives.

In the hug of temporariness, there is a significant freedom. The acknowledgment that everything is in a steady condition of motion welcomes us to deliver connections and embrace the consistently unfurling present second. It is an excursion of give up, an acquiescence to the patterns of life that convey us forward on the stream of time.

In this acquiescence, there is flexibility. The capacity to adjust and stream with the changing ebbs and flows of life permits us to explore difficulties with a feeling of composure. Like a tree that curves notwithstanding a tempest, we track down strength in our adaptability and that's what the figuring out, at last, the seasons will change, and new cycles will start.

The insight of seasons and cycles stretches out past the domain of simple perception. It is a challenge to partake effectively in the dance of presence. In developing consciousness of the cycles that shape our lives, we gain understanding into the examples that impact our considerations, feelings, and activities. This mindfulness turns into an amazing asset for self-awareness and change.

As we adjust ourselves to the patterns of our internal scene, we might find the common subjects and examples that shape our encounters. Similarly as the seasons impact the regular world, our convictions, propensities, and decisions establish the environment of our inward climate. With cognizant mindfulness, we can support the seeds of positive change, permitting them to flourish and thrive in the rich soil of our awareness.

The act of care turns into a directing light in exploring the seasons and patterns of our inner world. By securing ourselves right now, we become receptive to the unpretentious changes in our viewpoints and feelings. Care permits us to notice the changing scene of our internal experience without judgment, encouraging a feeling of lucidity and poise.

In the domain of connections, the consciousness of cycles turns into a compass for exploring the complicated elements between people. Similarly as the times of affection and association advance, so do the difficulties and open doors for development. By developing sympathy and understanding, we can explore the back and forth movement of associations with empathy and effortlessness.

The patterns of cultural and social advancement welcome us to ponder our aggregate process. The ascent and fall of developments, the undulating tides of progress and relapse, brief us to consider the inheritance we are molding for people in the future. In this reflection, there is a source of inspiration — a call to partake deliberately in the co-production of a world that praises the interconnectedness of all life.

Innovation, employed with care, can be an impetus for positive change. By perceiving the repetitive idea of development and outdated nature, we can saddle the force of innovation to address squeezing worldwide difficulties. The monetary cycles, with their true capacity for both success and imbalance, brief us to imagine new models of financial association that focus on manageability and inclusivity.

In the huge embroidery of reality, the patterns of the universe motivate a feeling of miracle and lowliness. The consciousness of our spot in the enormous dance welcomes us to develop a love for the interconnected snare of life that reaches out past the limits of our natural home. It is a call to stewardship, an acknowledgment that our activities echo through the texture of the universe.

In the dance of seasons and cycles, there is a basic amicability that rises above the bedlam of individual minutes. It is an ensemble of interconnected rhythms, an enormous expressive dance that unfurls with accuracy and beauty. As we adjust ourselves to this fantastic structure, we become dynamic members in the making of a world that praises the repeating idea of presence.

Taking everything into account, seasons and cycles are the strings that weave the complicated embroidery of our lives. From the changing times of the regular world to the vast cycles that oversee the universe, there is a significant interconnectedness that characterizes the human experience. In embracing the insight of temporariness and the magnificence inborn in the patterns of life, we find a guide for exploring the intricacies of our individual and aggregate excursions. As dynamic members in the dance of presence, we have the ability to develop care, flexibility, and a profound feeling of love for the interconnected snare of life that joins every one of us.

8.1 Discuss the importance of seasonal changes in the setting.

The significance of occasional changes in the setting couldn't possibly be more significant, as these changes assume a critical part in forming the climate, impacting environments, and influencing different parts of human existence. From the microcosm of a lawn nursery to the magnificence of huge scenes, occasional changes present a powerful musicality that influences vegetation, fauna, environment, and, surprisingly, the human mind.

One of the most apparent impacts of occasional changes is on the regular world, especially on vegetation. Spring, a time of recharging and resurrection, denotes the enlivening of lethargic plants. As temperatures climb, buds burst into sprout, and leaves spread out, arranging the scene with energetic varieties. This blast of life isn't simply a visual exhibition; it connotes the resumption of basic natural cycles like photosynthesis.

Photosynthesis, driven by daylight, is the key interaction through which plants convert carbon dioxide and water into glucose, delivering oxygen as a result. Spring, with its more drawn out days and expanded daylight, gives an ideal climate to this interaction. The overflow of sprouting blossoms and blooming trees isn't just a stylish wonder yet additionally a demonstration of the complex dance among seasons and the life-supporting cycles that support biological systems.

Summer follows, carrying with it warmth and broadened sunlight hours. This season is portrayed by the pinnacle of plant development and proliferation. The greenery that flourished in spring currently arrives at its apex, and numerous species produce products of the soil. These conceptive designs act as a crucial food hotspot for different creatures, shaping the groundwork of complicated food networks. The harmonious connection among pollinators and blossoming plants further shows the interconnectedness of occasional changes and environmental cycles.

Conversely, fall proclaims a period of progress. As temperatures cool and sunlight lessens, deciduous trees go through a dazzling change. The chlorophyll that once covered the genuine nature of leaves subsides, uncovering the energetic reds, oranges, and yellows of harvest time foliage. This change isn't just a visual scene yet additionally an essential transformation. Trees shed their passes on to save energy and assets during the crueler states of winter.

Winter, with its chilly temperatures and more limited days, denotes a time of lethargy for some plants. Deciduous trees stand uncovered, and perpetual plants retreat underground. The scene, once abounding with life, seems peaceful and torpid. Nonetheless, underneath the surface, essential cycles proceed. The virus is a characteristic lethargy trigger, permitting plants to ration energy until the arrival of additional good circumstances. This recurrent example of development, proliferation, lethargy, and reestablishment is fundamental for keeping up with the equilibrium and flexibility of environments.

Past the domain of greenery, occasional changes significantly influence the animals of the world collectively. Movement designs, regenerative cycles, and hibernation procedures are complicatedly connected to the evolving seasons. Numerous types of birds, for example, leave on amazing relocations, crossing mainlands to arrive at rearing or taking care of grounds. The accessibility of food, settling locales, and ideal weather patterns during explicit seasons impacts these transient ways of behaving.

Conceptive patterns of creatures are frequently synchronized with occasional changes, guaranteeing that posterity have the most obvious opportunity with regards to endurance. Spring, with its wealth of assets, is a typical time for some creatures to conceive an offspring or lay eggs. This essential timing improves the probability that youthful creatures will approach ample food sources during their basic beginning phases of advancement.

Hibernation is one more captivating variation to occasional changes. Numerous warm blooded creatures, from bears to hedgehogs, enter a condition of lethargy throughout the cold weather months when food is scant. This permits them to monitor energy and endure the unforgiving circumstances until the arrival of spring. The interconnected trap of these occasional ways of behaving exhibits the fragile equilibrium that exists inside environments.

The significance of occasional changes isn't restricted to the normal world; it stretches out into the domain of agribusiness and human vocation. Rural practices have generally been intently attached to the seasons, with ranchers depending on the repetitive examples of planting and gathering. The planning of planting is directed by the appearance of spring, guaranteeing that yields have adequate chance to develop and develop during the hotter months.

Gathering, then again, lines up with the overflow of pre-fall and early harvest time. The dependence on occasional changes in horticulture is profoundly imbued in customary cultivating practices and keeps on molding current cultivating schedules.

The shift away from this reliance, as found in certain types of indoor or nursery cultivating, highlights the extraordinary effect of innovation on our relationship with occasional cycles.

Additionally, the changing seasons significantly affect human prosperity and culture. Occasional emotional problem (Miserable), a sort of melancholy that happens occasionally, is a powerful illustration of the mental effect of changing light circumstances. Miserable is frequently connected to the decreased openness to regular daylight throughout the cold weather months, prompting side effects, for example, laziness, mind-set swings, and changes in rest designs.

On the other hand, the appearance of spring is related with a lift in state of mind and energy levels. This peculiarity highlights the complicated connection between our psychological prosperity and the evolving seasons. Socially, occasional changes have propelled innumerable ceremonies, celebrations, and customs across various social orders. The festival of spring celebrations, like Holi in India or the Japanese cherry bloom celebrations, mirrors a profound social appreciation for the reestablishment and essentialness related with the evolving seasons.

The imagery connected to occasional changes frequently tracks down articulation in craftsmanship, writing, and strict practices. The figurative meaning of spring as a period of reestablishment and trust, or winter as a time of reflection and torpidity, saturates human innovativeness. Specialists and authors draw motivation from the steadily moving scenes and airs that go with each season, making works that catch the embodiment of these worldly changes.

According to a climatic point of view, the changing seasons have expansive ramifications for weather conditions and environmental circumstances. The slant of the World's pivot comparative with its circle around the sun is answerable for the occasional varieties in environment. This pivotal slant makes various pieces of the Earth get fluctuating measures of sunlight based radiation over time, prompting the particular seasons we experience.

These climatic varieties, thus, impact worldwide weather conditions and peculiarities like storms, typhoons, and twisters. The changing seasons add to the many-sided dance of barometrical dissemination, affecting temperature, precipitation, and wind designs. Understanding these climatic movements is pivotal for anticipating and relieving the effects of outrageous climate occasions, which can have huge ramifications for networks and environments.

Moreover, the significance of occasional changes reaches out to the fragile equilibrium of Earth's biological systems. Biotic factors like plant development, creature ways of behaving, and microbial action are complicatedly connected to abiotic factors like temperature, daylight, and precipitation. Interruptions to these occasional examples, whether because of normal peculiarities or human exercises, can have flowing impacts on biodiversity, natural versatility, and the administrations environments give.

Human exercises, including deforestation, urbanization, and environmental change, can disturb the sensitive agreement of occasional examples. Deforestation, for example, adjusts the microclimates of woodlands, influencing the occasional ways of behaving of plants and creatures. Metropolitan intensity islands, made by the convergence of structures and asphalt, can compound temperature limits, disturbing the regular occasional rhythms that creatures depend on.

Environmental change, driven by human-prompted expansions in ozone depleting substance discharges, is modifying the examples of the seasons on a worldwide scale. Changes in temperature and precipitation designs, changing developing seasons, and more regular outrageous climate occasions are among the outcomes of a warming environment. These progressions present huge difficulties to biological systems, horticulture, and human social orders, stressing the interconnectedness of occasional cycles and more extensive natural issues.

All in all, the significance of occasional changes in the setting couldn't possibly be more significant. These repeating changes shape the regular world, impacting all that from plant development and creature conduct to atmospheric conditions and human prosperity. The interconnected trap of occasional examples highlights the fragile equilibrium that supports environments and societies the same. Perceiving and understanding the meaning of these progressions is fundamental for cultivating an economical relationship with the climate and moderating the effects of worldwide difficulties, for example, environmental change. As we explore the steadily moving scenes of the evolving seasons, we are helped to remember the significant interconnectedness of all life on The planet.

8.2 Explore how natural cycles affect various aspects of the world.

Normal cycles, natural for the texture of the Earth, weave a complicated embroidery that impacts horde parts of the world. From the cadenced dance of the seasons to the recurrent examples of environments and the enormous artful dance of divine bodies, these regular cycles shape the physical, natural, and, surprisingly, cultural elements of our planet. Understanding the significant effect of these cycles is critical for encouraging a comprehensive viewpoint on the interconnected frameworks that support life.

The most apparent and quick appearance of regular cycles is tracked down in the evolving seasons. The World's hub slant and its circle around the sun lead to the four unmistakable seasons: spring, summer, fall, and winter. Each season carries with it an interesting arrangement of climatic circumstances, sunlight terms, and biological peculiarities.

Spring, a time of recharging, marks the enlivening of life from winter's lethargy. As temperatures climb, plants answer by spreading out their leaves and delivering blooms. The scene changes into an uproar of varieties as blossoms sprout, and trees recover their lively foliage.

This explosion of life isn't just stylishly satisfying yet additionally fills in as a critical stage in the conceptive patterns of many plants.

Summer follows, described by longer days and hotter temperatures. The sun arrives at its pinnacle overhead, giving adequate energy to the development and development of vegetation. This season is inseparable from overflow, as harvests mature, and biological systems abound with life. The more extended light hours add to expanded photosynthesis, the interaction by which plants convert daylight into energy, molding the underpinning of the food web.

Pre-winter, a period of progress, brings cooler temperatures and more limited days. Deciduous trees go through a stupendous change as chlorophyll, the green shade liable for photosynthesis, separates, uncovering the clear tints of red, orange, and yellow in leaves. This season is frequently connected with harvests, as many products of the soil arrive at development, giving food to both natural life and people.

Winter, the last season in the cycle, is set apart by cool temperatures and, in certain locales, snowfall. Deciduous trees shed their leaves as a procedure to ration energy during the brutal circumstances. While the scene might seem torpid, fundamental biological cycles proceed. Many plants and creatures enter a time of torpidity, anticipating the arrival of additional great circumstances in the spring.

The effect of these occasional changes isn't bound to the normal world; it stretches out into the domains of farming, human wellbeing, and social practices. Customary farming practices have advanced to line up with the patterns of planting and reaping directed by the seasons. The planning of planting is critical to guarantee that harvests have adequate chance to develop and develop during the hotter months, improving yields.

Reaping, frequently connected with fall, is a climax of the developing season. The dependence on occasional cycles in horticulture is profoundly imbued in social practices and keeps on forming the livelihoods of ranchers around the world. As innovation and horticultural practices have progressed, a few locales have encountered a decoupling from conventional occasional examples through practices like indoor cultivating or tank-farming.

Notwithstanding farming, the changing seasons significantly affect human prosperity and wellbeing. Occasional Emotional Problem (Miserable), a kind of wretchedness connected to explicit seasons, is an illustration of the mental effect of occasional changes. Decreased openness to normal daylight throughout the cold weather months is accepted to add to the beginning of Miserable, featuring the complicated connection between natural elements and psychological well-being.

On the other hand, the appearance of spring and expanded daylight openness is related with further developed mind-set and energy levels. This peculiarity highlights the significance of the changing seasons in affecting circadian rhythms, rest wake cycles, and generally mental prosperity. Societies all over the planet have perceived and praised these occasional movements through celebrations, ceremonies, and customs that honor the recurrent idea of life.

Regular cycles stretch out past the yearly rhythm of seasons to incorporate more extensive natural cycles that support life on The planet. The carbon cycle, a principal biogeochemical process, directs the progression of carbon between the climate, seas, soil, and living creatures. Plants assume a focal part in this cycle by retaining carbon dioxide during photosynthesis and delivering oxygen, subsequently impacting air creation.

Human exercises, especially the consuming of non-renewable energy sources, deforestation, and modern cycles, have disturbed the sensitive equilibrium of the carbon cycle. Raised degrees of carbon dioxide in the air add to a dangerous atmospheric devation and environmental change, delineating how human-prompted modifications to regular cycles can have broad ramifications for the planet.

The water cycle, one more imperative interaction, oversees the development of water between the environment, seas, land, and living life forms. Vanishing, buildup, precipitation, spillover, and invasion are key parts of this cycle. Precipitation, as downpour or snow, recharges freshwater sources and supports environments. Changes in land use, like urbanization and deforestation, can adjust the regular progression of water, prompting issues like flooding or water shortage.

Biodiversity, the assortment of life on The planet, is complicatedly connected to normal cycles. Environments develop and adjust to occasional changes, and the accessibility of assets varies likewise. Movement designs, conceptive cycles, and ways of behaving of species are frequently synchronized with the evolving seasons. Disturbances to these cycles, whether because of environmental change, natural surroundings misfortune, or other anthropogenic elements, present dangers to biodiversity and biological steadiness.

In the domain of stargazing, heavenly bodies follow their own complex cycles, adding to the grandiose request. The Earth circles the sun in a normal example, bringing about the evolving seasons. The moon, in its circular circle around the Earth, goes through stages that impact flowing examples. The gravitational dance between the Earth, moon, and sun makes flowing powers that administer maritime tides, impacting marine biological systems and beach front scenes.

For a bigger scope, the existence patterns of stars, worlds, and, surprisingly, the actual universe are represented by infinite cycles.

Stars are brought into the world from shapeless billows of gas and residue, go through different phases of advancement, and in the long run either breakdown into dark openings or detonate as supernovae, cultivating space with the components essential for the arrangement of new stars and planets.

The universe extends, and systems travel through space, impacted by gravitational powers and vast expansion. These fantastic enormous cycles, happening on timescales that bantam human understanding, shape the actual texture of the universe. Investigating the profundities of room and understanding these divine cycles give experiences into the beginnings and fate of the universe.

Past the domains of cosmology and environment, cultural and social peculiarities are additionally impacted by regular cycles. Human social orders, from the beginning of time, have created schedules and customs that line up with the evolving seasons. Conventional rural social orders, specifically, stamped key occasions like planting, reap, and celebrations in view of the recurrent examples of nature.

In many societies, the changing seasons are entwined with legends, fables, and strict practices. The imagery of resurrection in spring, the wealth of summer, the gather of harvest time, and the contemplation of winter track down articulation in different social stories. Celebrations and services frequently match with occasional changes, mirroring the significant effect of normal cycles on human convictions and customs.

Mechanical headways and the globalization of social orders have, somewhat, weakened the immediate dependence on occasional examples for endurance. Current rural practices, helped by water system, nurseries, and hereditary alteration, can deliver crops outside their customary developing seasons. Essentially, the accessibility of labor and products is less compelled via occasional varieties in contemporary social orders.

Be that as it may, even in the time of mechanical ability, the effect of regular cycles endures. Environmental change, driven by human exercises, is modifying the examples of seasons, adding to outrageous climate occasions, changes in precipitation, and disturbances to biological systems. The results of these progressions resonate through worldwide food frameworks, water assets, and the weakness of networks to natural dangers.

The acknowledgment of the reliance between human exercises and normal cycles has prodded endeavors to foster maintainable practices. Ideas, for example, regenerative farming, which underscores working as one with normal biological systems, expect to reestablish and improve the strength of the land. Supportable ranger service rehearses, environmentally friendly power drives, and preservation endeavors are reactions to the comprehension that the prosperity of human social orders is complicatedly connected to the strength of the planet.

8.3 Highlight the symbolism and impact of recurring patterns.

Repeating designs, woven into the texture of presence, convey significant imagery and apply a significant effect on the world we occupy. Whether appeared in the cyclic rhythms of nature, the complicated dance of divine bodies, or the dull themes inside human societies, these examples convey more profound implications and shape how we might interpret life. Inspecting the imagery and effect of repeating designs permits us to unwind the strings of implying that interface different parts of our reality.

The evolving seasons, maybe the most obvious and generally perceived repeating design, epitomize rich imagery and apply a significant effect on the normal world.

Spring, with its blooming blossoms and lively vegetation, represents restoration, resurrection, and the repeating idea of life. The development of life from the torpidity of winter matches the perpetual expectation for fresh starts and the flexibility intrinsic despite challenges.

Summer, described by warmth and overflow, is a time of development and realization. It represents the pinnacle of imperativeness and the satisfaction of potential. The long days and abundant harvests mirror the compensations of tirelessness and exertion, underlining the interconnectedness of human undertakings with the more extensive patterns of nature.

Pre-winter, a period of progress set apart by the changing shades of falling leaves, conveys emblematic importance. The shedding of leaves by deciduous trees addresses giving up, it is not generally expected to deliver what. This demonstration of shedding, while apparently an introduction to lethargy, is a fundamental stage for restoration and recovery, repeating subjects of fleetingness and the recurrent idea of life.

Winter, with its chilly temperatures and desolate scenes, represents thoughtfulness and torpidity. It is a time of rest and reflection, where the earth takes a relief before the pattern of recharging starts once more. The imagery of winter addresses the significance of tranquility and calm examination in the general beat of life.

Past their representative implications, the changing seasons apply a substantial effect on environments, horticulture, and human prosperity. The cyclic examples of plant development and propagation, affected by the seasons, structure the underpinning of food networks and biodiversity. Farming practices, lined up with occasional cycles, shape planting and collecting schedules, directing the accessibility of yields and impacting worldwide food frameworks.

Human wellbeing and prosperity are additionally complicatedly associated with the evolving seasons. The peculiarity of Occasional Emotional Issue (Miserable), a kind of sadness related with explicit seasons, highlights the effect of light openness and occasional changes on psychological wellness.

Alternately, the mental lift frequently knowledgeable about the appearance of spring mirrors the advantageous connection between human feelings and the common habitat.

In the divine domain, the repetitive examples of the moon and the sun add to imagery and effect that rise above social and worldly limits. The moon, with its coming and going stages, has been a wellspring of motivation and imagery across different societies. The full moon, with its brilliant sparkle, is frequently connected with light, edification, and the disclosing of stowed away insights. On the other hand, the new moon, covered in haziness, means starting points, secret, and the potential for new undertakings.

The sun, a divine steady in our day to day routines, goes through its own common example of rising and setting. The imagery related with the sun shifts across societies however frequently envelops subjects of life, essentialness, and enlightenment. The rising sun is a general image of fresh starts, trust, and the unyielding walk of time. The sunset, with its plummet into obscurity, addresses consummation, reflection, and the repeating idea of presence.

These divine examples, past their representative weight, impact normal peculiarities like tides, seasons, and environment. The gravitational dance between the Earth, moon, and sun brings about flowing powers that administer maritime tides. The pivotal slant of the Earth comparative with its circle around the sun prompts the evolving seasons, affecting worldwide weather conditions and biological cycles. Understanding and outfitting the impact of these heavenly examples have been vital in fields like agribusiness, route, and timekeeping.

In the microcosm of human societies, repeating designs manifest in images, legends, and customs that rise above ages. Model images, like the circle, twisting, or mandala, exemplify the idea of repetitive examples and solidarity. The circle, specifically, is an image of completeness, endlessness, and the boundless idea of time. Mandalas, mathematical examples with a main issue, are tracked down in different social and strict practices, addressing the universe and the repeating idea of life.

Folklores from various societies frequently include repeating themes and model stories that reflect the cyclic rhythms of nature. The legend's excursion, a story design distinguished by Joseph Campbell, is a common theme tracked down in fantasies across societies. It follows the legend as they leave on an experience, face preliminaries, accomplish change, and return to their local area with freshly discovered intelligence. This cyclic account reflects the repeating examples of life, passing, and resurrection.

Customs and services, inserted with emblematic significance, as often as possible show repeating designs. Soul changing experiences, checking huge life advances like birth, inception, marriage, and passing, frequently follow an organized example.

These customs give a feeling of request and congruity, underlining the recurrent idea of human encounters. They act as aggregate articulations of social personality, interfacing people to their legacy and the immortal rhythms of presence.

Language itself, a key part of human culture, displays repeating designs as semantic designs, rhythms, and themes. The reiteration of sounds, words, and expressions in verse and writing adds to the stylish excellence of language and stresses subjects and feelings. The cyclic idea of narrating, with its original characters and account structures, reverberates across societies and ages, rising above individual encounters to associate with general human subjects.

In the domain of visual expressions, repeating designs are utilized for representative and tasteful purposes. Mandala craftsmanship, with its complicated mathematical examples emanating from an essential issue, is a common theme in different societies. Mathematical examples, for example, the Fibonacci arrangement or the Brilliant Proportion, show up in workmanship and engineering, mirroring the innate request and agreement tracked down in nature.

The effect of repeating designs reaches out to the space of innovation and development. The iterative cycle, described by the reiteration of configuration, testing, and refinement, is a crucial methodology in designing and item improvement. This iterative example considers ceaseless improvement, variation to evolving conditions, and the refinement of arrangements over the long haul.

In the field of data innovation, calculations frequently depend on repeating examples and circles to effectively execute undertakings. The idea of recursion, where a capability calls itself in a dull way, is a major programming rule that reflects the repeating idea of many cycles in nature and human undertakings.

Financial cycles, with their examples of development, compression, and recuperation, apply a significant effect on social orders and worldwide business sectors. The win and fail periods of monetary cycles impact work, speculation, and purchaser conduct. The repeating idea of monetary examples highlights the interconnectedness of worldwide monetary frameworks and the difficulties of accomplishing feasible development.

Natural cycles, for example, supplement cycles in biological systems, assume a basic part in keeping up with environmental equilibrium. The nitrogen cycle, for example, includes the rehashed cycles of nitrogen obsession, nitrification, and denitrification. These cyclic cycles guarantee the accessibility of fundamental supplements for plant development while forestalling the gathering of overabundance nitrogen, which can adversely affect biological systems.

The effect of repeating designs on human comprehension and discernment is a subject of interest for clinicians and neuroscientists. Design acknowledgment, a mental cycle that includes recognizing consistencies in tangible info, is a key part of human knowledge. The capacity to perceive repeating designs permits people to explore their current circumstance, make forecasts, and structure mental models of the world.

In the area of brain science, the idea of models, proposed via Carl Jung, features repeating images and examples in the aggregate oblivious. Models, like the legend, the mother, or the shadow, are general images that reverberate across societies and are communicated in fantasies, dreams, and imaginative manifestations. Understanding these model examples gives bits of knowledge into the firmly established parts of human experience and the common representative language that rises above individual contrasts.

The effect of repeating designs on human way of behaving is clear in the domain of propensities, schedules, and cultural standards. People frequently float towards recognizable examples and schedules, tracking down solace and soundness in the consistency of dull ways of behaving. Cultural standards, built up through social practices and assumptions, frequently show repeating designs that shape aggregate way of behaving and esteems.

The idea of social cycles, proposed by antiquarians and sociologists, recommends that social orders go through repeating examples of development, decline, and reestablishment. The ascent and fall of civilizations, set apart by patterns of development, stagnation, and breakdown, highlight the recurrent idea of authentic cycles.

The effect of repeating designs stretches out across different elements of human life, impacting individual way of behaving, cultural designs, social articulations, and, surprisingly, the normal world. These examples, whether appeared in cycles, rhythms, or reiterations, add to the texture of our encounters, forming how we see and connect with the world. Investigating the effect of repeating designs offers experiences into the elements that oversee our lives and the significant outcomes that rise out of these recurrent peculiarities.

One of the most unavoidable and prompt effects of repeating designs is seen in individual propensities and schedules. Human way of behaving is intrinsically molded by the reiteration of day to day exercises, shaping schedules that give a feeling of design and consistency. From wake-up routines to sleep time schedules, these examples add to productivity, mental prosperity, and a feeling of control in exploring the intricacies of day to day existence.

The impact of repeating designs on individual propensities stretches out to the domain of mastering and ability improvement. The most common way of gaining new abilities frequently includes rehashed practice and support, making brain processes that work with dominance. Schooling systems, as well, are organized around repeating examples of classes, semesters, and assessments, giving a structure to learning and information securing.

On a cultural level, repeating designs manifest in the repetitive idea of financial cycles. The effect of monetary examples, described by times of extension, withdrawal, and recuperation, resounds through networks, affecting business rates, purchaser spending, and generally flourishing. The rhythmic movement of monetary cycles add to the dynamism and versatility of social orders, forming examples of creation, utilization, and development.

The repeating idea of monetary examples additionally highlights the interconnectedness of worldwide business sectors. The waves of financial changes in a single region of the planet can have expansive results, influencing exchange, speculation, and international elements. The effect of repeating financial examples requires versatile procedures, strength, and strategy intercessions to alleviate the impacts of slumps and encourage maintainable development.

Inside the domain of ecological science, the effect of repeating designs is apparent in regular cycles, for example, the water cycle, carbon cycle, and supplement cycles. These fundamental cycles administer the development of water, supplements, and gases through environments, supporting life and keeping up with biological equilibrium. Interruptions to these cycles, whether brought about by human exercises or regular occasions, can have flowing consequences for biodiversity, soil richness, and the wellbeing of biological systems.

The water cycle, for instance, includes the rehashed cycles of vanishing, buildup, precipitation, and overflow. This repetitive example guarantees the recharging of freshwater sources, the sustenance of vegetation, and the food of amphibian environments. Human exercises that modify land use, like deforestation or urbanization, can upset the regular progression of water and add to issues like flooding or water shortage.

With regards to environmental change, the effect of repeating designs is especially articulated. Changes in worldwide temperature designs, precipitation cycles, and outrageous climate occasions are ascribed to human-actuated adjustments in the World's environment framework. The acknowledgment of these disturbances highlights the desperation of tending to the underlying drivers of environmental change and executing techniques for variation and alleviation.

Social articulations, as well, are profoundly impacted by repeating designs. Images, themes, and model accounts frequently return in workmanship, writing, and folklore across different societies and verifiable periods. The effect of these repetitive examples lies in their capacity to convey widespread subjects, reverberate with human encounters, and rise above worldly and geological limits.

Model images, like the legend's excursion or the theme of the enormous cycle, act as strong vehicles for conveying significant insights and experiences. These common examples tap into the aggregate oblivious, as proposed by clinician Carl Jung, giving a common language of images that interfaces people across societies and ages.

The effect of original examples is apparent in the getting through reverberation of fantasies, fables, and strict stories that keep on molding human getting it.

The effect of repeating designs on social practices is likewise reflected in customs, services, and celebrations. Soul changing experiences, checking critical life changes, frequently follow an organized example including partition, inception, and fuse. These repetitive examples give a feeling of progression, meaning, and mutual personality, encouraging a common perspective of the repeating idea of life.

In the domain of language and correspondence, repeating designs add to the wealth and expressiveness of human articulation. Scholarly gadgets like reiteration, cadence, and rhyme are utilized to make noteworthy and effective encounters for perusers or audience members. The effect of repeating designs in language stretches out to manner of speaking, verse, and narrating, where the purposeful utilization of redundancy can summon feelings, underline subjects, and improve the general tasteful allure.

The effect of repeating designs is likewise obvious in mechanical advancements and the iterative idea of logical request. The iterative cycle, described by the redundancy of configuration, testing, and refinement, is principal to headways in designing and item improvement. This repetitive example takes into consideration constant improvement, variation to evolving conditions, and the refinement of arrangements after some time.

In the domain of data innovation, calculations frequently depend on repeating examples and circles to proficiently execute errands. The idea of recursion, where a capability calls itself in a tedious way, is a crucial programming rule that reflects the repeating idea of many cycles in nature and human undertakings. The effect of these common examples in innovation is extraordinary, affecting the improvement of computerized reasoning, AI, and information examination.

The effect of repeating designs on human insight and discernment is a subject of interest for clinicians and neuroscientists. Design acknowledgment, a mental cycle that includes distinguishing normalities in tangible info, is major to human knowledge.

The capacity to perceive repeating designs permits people to explore their current circumstance, make expectations, and structure mental models of the world.

The effect of repeating designs on human perception is apparent in the peculiarity of pareidolia, where people see recognizable examples or significant pictures in arbitrary upgrades. This propensity to recognize designs, whether in cloud arrangements or conceptual workmanship, addresses the natural human tendency to force request and significance on the apparent tumult of the world.

Cultural designs and establishments, as well, are formed by repeating designs. Social cycles, proposed by students of history and sociologists, recommend that social orders go through rehashing examples of development, decline, and reestablishment. The ascent and fall of civic establishments, set apart by patterns of development, stagnation, and breakdown, highlight the recurrent idea of authentic cycles. Understanding these social cycles gives experiences into the elements that add to the strength or weakness of social orders over the long run.

The effect of repeating designs on cultural standards and aggregate way of behaving is apparent in the recurrent idea of social patterns and forms. Patterns in design, music, workmanship, and mainstream society frequently follow repeating examples of ubiquity, immersion, and possible downfall. The recurrent idea of social patterns mirrors the unique interchange between advancement, impersonation, and the aggregate inclinations of society.

The effect of repeating designs on cultural standards stretches out to the domain of administration and political cycles. Political frameworks frequently go through repeating examples of strength, change, and transformation. Decisions, strategy cycles, and cultural assumptions add to the cadenced examples of political life. The effect of these repetitive examples is felt in the forming of regulations, foundations, and the general direction of cultural turn of events.

Chapter 9

Maintaining Harmony

Keeping up with congruity in one's life requires a fragile harmony between different perspectives, enveloping connections, work, individual prosperity, and more extensive cultural associations. The quest for concordance frequently starts with mindfulness and a cognizant work to comprehend and deal with the various features of one's presence. It is a continuous excursion, formed by encounters, decisions, and the capacity to adjust to the consistently changing elements of life.

In the domain of individual connections, concordance is developed through compelling correspondence and sympathy. The underpinning of any solid relationship lies in shared understanding and regard. Listening effectively to others' viewpoints, recognizing their sentiments, and putting oneself out there really add to an agreeable association. Struggle is unavoidable in any relationship, yet it is how clashes are taken care of that characterizes the general amicability. Embracing split the difference, figuring out some shared interest, and gaining from conflicts encourage development and reinforce the connection between people.

Besides, it is foremost to keep up with agreement inside oneself. This includes a comprehensive way to deal with prosperity incorporating physical, mental, and close to home aspects. A sound way of life that integrates normal activity, a decent eating regimen, and adequate rest lays the basis for actual prosperity. Mental prosperity is sustained through care rehearses, for example, contemplation and self-reflection, which assist with overseeing pressure and develop a positive outlook. The capacity to appreciate people on a profound level assumes a critical part in understanding and managing one's feelings, cultivating versatility, and building inward congruity.

Balance between serious and fun activities is one more urgent part chasing after in general congruity. The requests of a cutting edge, high speed workplace can some of the time lead to burnout and burden on private connections. Defining limits, focusing on undertakings, and setting aside a few minutes for unwinding are fundamental methodologies to work out some kind of harmony among expert and individual life.

Besides, finding reason and fulfillment in one's work contributes essentially to a feeling of satisfaction, adding to the general concordance throughout everyday life.

Past individual circles, cultural congruity includes an aggregate work to make an equitable and comprehensive local area. This involves perceiving and regarding variety, advancing fairness, and tending to social shameful acts. Thoughtful gestures, sympathy, and compassion are the structure blocks of an agreeable society. At the point when people by and large make progress toward the prosperity, everything being equal, cultural congruity thrives, establishing a positive and steady climate for everybody.

Developing congruity likewise includes a careful way to deal with innovation and its effect on day to day existence. While innovation has without a doubt brought comfort and network, its unreasonable use can prompt separation from the current second and disturb individual connections. Finding some kind of harmony by defining limits on screen time, encouraging eye to eye collaborations, and rehearsing computerized care adds to a more amicable mix of innovation into day to day existence.

Ecological agreement is a frequently disregarded however basic part of the more extensive quest for balance. The sensitive equilibrium of biological systems, environment, and biodiversity straightforwardly influences human prosperity. Taking on feasible works on, decreasing carbon impressions, and upholding for natural protection add to an amicable concurrence with the planet. Perceiving the interconnectedness of every single living being and the climate encourages a feeling of obligation for the prosperity of the Earth.

Schooling assumes a critical part in forming people and networks toward an agreeable future. Balanced training gives information as well as imparts upsides of sympathy, resistance, and understanding. By advancing decisive reasoning and cultivating a worldwide point of view, schooling turns into an amazing asset in building spans across different societies and points of view, adding to a more agreeable world.

The quest for concordance isn't without its difficulties. Life is intrinsically unique, introducing unexpected hindrances and vulnerabilities. Nonetheless, it is definitively despite misfortune that the genuine trial of one's obligation to amicability arises. Flexibility, versatility, and a positive outlook become fundamental credits in exploring the back and forth movement of life. Embracing change as an unavoidable piece of the excursion and gaining from difficulties add to self-awareness and a persevering through feeling of congruity.

All in all, keeping up with concordance is a complex and deep rooted try that envelops individual connections, individual prosperity, cultural associations, innovation, the climate, training, and the capacity to explore life's difficulties with versatility and flexibility. It is a constant course of self-disclosure, development, and careful living. By encouraging concordance inside ourselves, in our connections, and inside the more extensive local area, we add to a more adjusted and interconnected reality where the prosperity of everything is esteemed and maintained. Eventually, the quest for congruity is a common excursion that rises above individual limits, making an embroidery of interconnected lives taking a stab at an amicable concurrence.

9.1 Summarize key elements for creating and maintaining a harmonious setting.

Making and keeping an agreeable setting is a diverse undertaking that includes a fragile equilibrium of different key components. These components, when painstakingly considered and coordinated, add to a climate where people can flourish, connections can prosper, and a feeling of prosperity wins. From the actual parts of the space to the social elements at play, every part assumes a urgent part as one. In this investigation, we will dig into the major perspectives that add to the creation and food of an agreeable setting.

At the center of any amicable setting lies the actual climate. The plan and design of a space significantly affect its inhabitants. Smart thought should be given to elements, for example, lighting, variety plans, and spatial course of action. Normal light, for example, has been displayed to impact temperament and efficiency emphatically. A sufficiently bright space improves perceivability as well as makes an inviting air. Additionally, the selection of varieties can inspire explicit feelings and set the vibe for the climate. Warm tones like reds and yellows can make a feeling of warmth and energy, while cool tones like blues and greens might cultivate a quieting and tranquil climate.

Spatial game plan is one more basic part of the actual climate. The design ought to be helpful for the exercises occurring inside the space. Whether it's an office, a home, or a shared region, the plan of furniture and different components ought to work with simplicity of development and connection. Open, streaming spaces can empower cooperation and correspondence, while clear cut zones can give a feeling of design and association.

Past the substantial parts of the actual climate, the consolidation of components that enticement for the faculties is fundamental for making an agreeable setting. Tastefully satisfying craftsmanship, calming music, and charming fragrances can all add to a positive environment. The tangible experience of a space goes past visual style; it envelops a comprehensive methodology that connects with people on different levels.

Similarly significant is the requirement for usefulness and common sense in the plan of an amicable setting. The space ought to be coordinated such that supports its planned reason. Mess and complication can prompt pressure and interruption, frustrating the general congruity of the climate. Sufficient capacity arrangements, ergonomic furnishings, and productive utilization of room all add to a very much planned and useful setting.

Moving past the actual climate, the social elements inside a setting assume a vital part in laying out and keeping up with congruity. Correspondence is a foundation of any sound relationship, and this turns out as expected in both individual and expert settings. Open and straightforward correspondence cultivates understanding, decreases clashes, and fortifies associations among people.

In an agreeable setting, people feel appreciated and esteemed. Undivided attention is a vital part of successful correspondence. At the point when individuals feel that their viewpoints and points of view are regarded, it develops a feeling of common comprehension and advances joint effort. Furthermore, cultivating a culture of inclusivity and variety adds to a rich embroidery of thoughts and encounters, upgrading the general energy of the setting.

The foundation of clear assumptions and limits is one more essential part of social elements inside an agreeable setting. Whether it's a family, a group, or a local area, having distinct assumptions oversees relational connections. Clear limits give a feeling of safety and assist with forestalling errors or clashes that might emerge from muddled or implicit guidelines.

Trust is a foundation of amicable connections. Assembling and keeping up with trust requires consistency, dependability, and respectability. At the point when people can trust each other, it makes a feeling of mental security, taking into consideration transparent correspondence. Trust is a delicate yet essential component that, once broken, can be trying to reestablish. In this manner, it should be sustained and focused on in any setting seeking to keep up with agreement.

Compromise abilities are fundamental chasing concordance. Clashes are a characteristic piece of human connection, yet the way that they are tended to can either reinforce or sabotage the general concordance of a setting. People furnished with viable compromise abilities can explore conflicts with compassion and understanding, finding arrangements that are helpful together.

Notwithstanding relational connections, authority assumes a urgent part in molding the social elements of a setting. An amicable setting benefits from pioneers who encapsulate characteristics like compassion, lowliness, and a certifiable worry for the prosperity of others. Administration that is grounded in these standards cultivates a positive and comprehensive culture, rousing trust and collaboration among colleagues.

Developing a feeling of local area is fundamental in different settings, from private neighborhoods to work environments. A solid feeling of local area makes an encouraging group of people, cultivating a common feeling of having a place and association. Exercises and drives that unite individuals, whether through get-togethers, group building exercises, or local area projects, add to a firm and amicable climate.

Chasing agreement, it is significant to perceive and resolve issues of force elements and imbalance. Whether in a familial setting or a bigger cultural setting, recognizing and attempting to redress lopsided characteristics is essential for encouraging a comprehensive and amicable climate. This includes destroying foundational obstructions and advancing equivalent open doors for all people, no matter what their experience or personality.

The idea of care holds critical worth in making and keeping an amicable setting. Care includes being completely present at the time, developing consciousness of one's viewpoints and feelings without judgment. Rehearsing care can add to a feeling of inward harmony and poise, which, thusly, decidedly impacts the general environment of a setting. Careful people are in many cases more receptive to their environmental elements and better prepared to deal with stressors in a cool headed way.

An amicable setting is one that qualities and focuses on the prosperity of its occupants. This incorporates actual wellbeing, mental prosperity, and profound flexibility. Giving assets and backing to people to keep a solid way of life adds to a general positive environment. Health programs, admittance to wellness offices, and drives that advance a sound balance between fun and serious activities all assume a part in establishing a climate that upholds the comprehensive prosperity of its tenants.

Adaptability and versatility are fundamental characteristics notwithstanding change. The capacity to explore vulnerabilities and adjust to advancing conditions is urgent for keeping up with amicability. Whether it's a change in the expert scene, changes in relational peculiarities, or cultural changes, an amicable setting embraces adaptability and urges people to move toward change with flexibility and a positive outlook.

Praising accomplishments and achievements, both individual and group, is a strong method for building up a feeling of achievement and pride inside a setting. Acknowledgment and affirmation for an incredible piece of handiwork, whether through proper honors or basic articulations of appreciation, add to a positive and spurring air. Commending triumphs cultivates a culture of consolation and builds up the possibility that singular commitments are esteemed.

Schooling and nonstop learning are fundamental to the supported congruity of a setting. Giving open doors to people to obtain new abilities, grow their insight, and participate in private and expert improvement adds to a dynamic and ground breaking climate. Learning encourages development, versatility, and advancement, fundamental characteristics for exploring the intricacies of the present world.

All in all, the creation and upkeep of an agreeable setting require a comprehensive methodology that envelops the actual climate, social elements, and individual prosperity. Insightful plan, viable correspondence, trust, compromise abilities, and a pledge to inclusivity are among the key components that add to congruity. Pioneers, whether in a family, local area, or hierarchical setting, assume a pivotal part in forming the way of life and elements of a setting.

Cultivating a feeling of local area, tending to drive uneven characters, and elevating care add to a good and comprehensive air. Focusing on the prosperity of people through drives that help physical, mental, and profound wellbeing is fundamental. Adaptability, flexibility, and a readiness to embrace change are characteristics that support congruity notwithstanding developing conditions.

Commending accomplishments and cultivating a culture of persistent learning add to a positive and ground breaking climate. At last, the quest for congruity is a continuous and cooperative exertion that requires an aggregate obligation to making a space where people can flourish, connections can thrive, and the general prosperity of the local area is focused on.

9.2 Discuss how authors can ensure consistency and coherence throughout the narrative.

Keeping up with consistency and rationality in an account is a central part of viable narrating. Writers endeavor to make a consistent and drawing in understanding experience, where the plot unfurls sensibly, characters develop legitimately, and the general story structure stays strong. Accomplishing this requires cautious regard for different components, including plot advancement, character depiction, composing style, and topical intelligence.

One of the essential contemplations for creators looking for story consistency is the improvement of a very much organized plot. The storyline ought to unfurl in a consistent grouping, with occasions and improvements that line up with the laid out world and character elements. A reasonable and cognizant plot guarantees that perusers can follow the story curve without disarray, permitting them to put resources into the story and expect its movement.

In making a predictable plot, creators frequently start with a strong blueprint. This guide gives a system to the story, framing key occasions, character curves, and topical components. While imagination and immediacy have their position in the creative cycle, having a central construction assists creators with remaining on track and stay away from plot openings or confusions that might think twice about generally rationality of the story.

Character consistency is similarly urgent. Characters are the core of any story, and their activities, responses, and improvement should line up with their laid out attributes and inspirations. Perusers structure associations with characters in light of their credibility and appeal, and any deviation from laid out character qualities can upset the account's cognizance. Creators should be aware of character coherence, guaranteeing that the decisions and ways of behaving of their characters stay consistent with their laid out characters.

Discourse is a critical device for conveying character qualities and keeping up with consistency. Each character ought to have a particular voice, and their exchange ought to mirror their singular peculiarities, discourse examples, and points of view. Reliable portrayal through discourse improves trustworthiness as well as helps perusers in recognizing characters, adding to a more vivid understanding experience.

Past individual person consistency, creators should likewise think about the elements and connections between characters. Communications ought to be true and in accordance with the laid out associations between characters. Consistency in connections adds to the general lucidness of the story, making a trap of associations that perusers can explore with certainty.

Setting assumes a critical part in story consistency. Whether the story unfurls in a clearly depicted dream domain or a fastidiously explored verifiable period, the setting should stay steady all through the story. Changes in the climate ought to be made sense of or legitimized, and any world-building components presented ought to line up with the laid out rules and rationale of the imaginary world. Consistency in setting adds to the vivid nature of the account, permitting perusers to actually imagine and draw in with the story more.

Language and composing style are extra factors that influence account consistency. Writers should keep a steady tone and style all through the story, guaranteeing a durable understanding encounter. Unexpected changes in language or composing style can be shaking for perusers and may upset the progression of the account. Whether the tone is formal, casual, elucidating, or compact, it ought to stay reliable except if deliberate movements fill a particular story need.

Topical rationality is one more basic thought for creators expecting to make a strong story. The topics investigated in the story, whether they rotate around affection, misfortune, character, or cultural issues, ought to be woven consistently into the texture of the account. Consistency in topical components adds to a brought together and effective narrating experience, permitting perusers to investigate further layers of significance inside the story.

Anticipating and callbacks are powerful devices for upgrading topical and story consistency. Presenting components right off the bat in the story that become critical later on makes a feeling of union as well as remunerations mindful perusers. Callbacks, or references to prior occasions or subjects, effectively support the account's coherence and feature the interconnectedness of various story components.

Viable pacing is essential for keeping up with story cognizance. The musicality at which situation transpire ought to line up with the general tone and classification of the story. Abrupt changes in pacing can disturb the stream and lucidness of the story, leaving perusers muddled. Writers should think about the pacing of individual scenes, parts, and the story overall to guarantee an even and connecting with understanding experience.

Updating and altering are fundamental stages in the creative cycle for accomplishing account consistency. Creators ought to return to their work with a basic eye, searching for irregularities in plot, character, setting, and subject. Input from beta perusers or editors can give significant experiences, assisting creators with distinguishing regions where the story might need rationality or where irregularities might emerge.

It's vital to take note of that accomplishing consistency and intelligence doesn't mean dispensing with all astonishments or deviations from the normal. Innovativeness frequently flourishes with flightiness, and first rate unexpected developments or character improvements can add profundity to a story. Nonetheless, these components ought to be coordinated nicely and such that upgrades, as opposed to cheapens, the general intelligibility of the story.

All in all, creators face the continuous test of guaranteeing consistency and rationality all through their accounts. This includes careful regard for different components, including plot advancement, character depiction, setting, language, topical cognizance, and pacing. A very much organized plot gives an establishment to the story, while steady portrayal and bona fide exchange add to the credibility of characters. Setting ought with stay stable and comply to laid out rules, and topical components ought to be flawlessly woven into the account texture.

Language and composing style ought to keep up with consistency, and the utilization of portending and callbacks can improve topical rationality. Pacing, a critical component of narrating, ought to line up with the general tone and classification of the story. Modifying and altering assume imperative parts in recognizing and correcting irregularities, and criticism from others can give significant viewpoints. At last, accomplishing story consistency requires a cautious harmony among imagination and congruity, bringing about a convincing and vivid perusing experience for the crowd.

9.3 Explore potential challenges and solutions in maintaining harmony in the world-building process.

World-building is a perplexing and unpredictable cycle that creators embrace to make vivid and trustworthy fictitious universes. Whether making a dream domain, a modern culture, or an other verifiable setting, the undertaking of building a lucid and amicable world presents both inventive open doors and difficulties. This investigation digs into the potential difficulties creators might look on the planet building process and inspects different answers for conquer these obstacles, guaranteeing a durable and connecting with story.

One of the underlying difficulties in world-building emerges from the need to lay out a steady and obvious arrangement of rules overseeing the made up universe. This incorporates the laws of physical science, enchantment frameworks, social standards, and cultural designs. Irregularities in these central components can sabotage the perusers' willingness to accept some far-fetched situations and cheapen the general union of the account. To address this test, creators should carefully frame the guidelines and boundaries of their reality, guaranteeing that each viewpoint lines up with the laid out structure.

An answer for this challenge lies in making a complete world-building book of scriptures. This report fills in as a source of perspective aide for the creator, specifying the complexities of the made up world. It remembers data for the geology, history, societies, advances, and any fantastical components extraordinary to the setting. Consistently counseling this world-building book of scriptures assists writers with keeping up with consistency and stay away from inconsistencies all through the creative cycle.

Social soundness is one more huge test in world-building, particularly while managing assorted social orders inside the made up universe. Each culture ought to have its own particular qualities, including language, customs, customs, and conviction frameworks. Irregularities in the depiction of societies can prompt social generalizations or an absence of profundity, decreasing the wealth of the world. Creators should concentrate intensely on understanding the subtleties of each culture they make and guarantee that these components stay consistent with their laid out profiles.

To defeat the test of social cognizance, creators can take part in careful examination and draw motivation from true societies. This adds validness to the imaginary social orders as well as helps in keeping away from coincidental social allocation or distortion. Working together with awareness perusers from different foundations can give significant experiences and guarantee that social portrayals are deferential and precise.

Adjusting composition and drenching is a sensitive undertaking in world-building. A lot of work can overpower perusers with data, hindering the story stream, while too little might leave them confused and attempting to figure out the imaginary world. Finding some kind of harmony is fundamental for keeping up with peruser commitment and guaranteeing that the world-building improves, instead of blocks, the narrating.

One compelling answer for this challenge is incorporating world-building naturally into the story. As opposed to introducing data in extended article dumps, writers can uncover subtleties continuously through character collaborations, discourse, and the unfurling of occasions. Displaying the world through the characters' viewpoints permits perusers to investigate and find out about the setting as a fundamental piece of the story, encouraging a feeling of disclosure and submersion.

Consistency in the progression of time is a test that frequently emerges in world-building, especially while managing mind boggling timetables, verifiable occasions, or the pacing of mechanical headways. Conflicting timetables can prompt sensible irregularities and upset the's comprehension perusers might interpret the world's advancement. Creators should lay out a reasonable timetable for their imaginary universe and stick to it all through the story.

Making a point by point timetable or sequence of critical occasions on the planet building process assists creators with keeping up with consistency in the progression of time. This timetable ought to incorporate key verifiable occasions, social movements, and mechanical turns of events. Consistently referring to the timetable during the creative cycle guarantees that the story lines up with the laid out transient system, forestalling unintentional chronological errors or irregularities.

Keeping up with concordance in the power elements of a made up world represents one more test for creators. Whether managing political designs, otherworldly progressive systems, or social classes, irregularities in power elements can prompt an absence of credibility and sabotage the story's soundness. Creators should cautiously lay out the standards administering power inside their universes and guarantee that these elements stay predictable.

An answer for this challenge includes a fastidious investigation of the power structures inside the imaginary universe. Figuring out the circulation of force, the instruments of administration, and the variables that impact authority permits creators to depict reasonable and inside predictable power elements. Also, taking into account the results of force awkward nature on various cultural gatherings upgrades the profundity and intricacy of the world.

Keeping up with etymological intelligibility is a test, particularly while concocting new dialects or tongues for fictitious societies. Conflicting utilization of language or phonetic advancement can make disarray and upset the vivid experience for perusers.

Creators should lay out reliable etymological guidelines and examples inside the world, guaranteeing that the language mirrors the social and authentic setting.

To address this test, creators can foster a language guide or glossary that frames the sentence structure, jargon, and phonetic characteristics of the imaginary dialects. Reliably applying these semantic guidelines all through the account adds to the realness of the world. Also, consolidating phonetic advancement after some time, reflecting certifiable language changes, adds profundity to the world-building.

The test of keeping up with topical rationality includes guaranteeing that the all-encompassing subjects of the account line up with the world-building components. Irregularities between the subjects investigated and the world's social, cultural, or mysterious perspectives can make a disconnected understanding encounter. Creators should cautiously coordinate topical components into the texture of the world, permitting these subjects to reverberate all through the account.

One answer for this challenge is to lay out areas of strength for an establishment during the world-building process. Recognizing the center subjects that the account plans to investigate helps guide the improvement of the imaginary world. Coordinating these subjects into the social, authentic, and mystical parts of the world guarantees that each component contributes firmly to the all-encompassing story subjects.

Tending to the test of mechanical consistency is vital, particularly in speculative fiction where trend setting innovations or mysterious frameworks are common. Irregularities in the application or constraints of innovation can disturb the perusers' willingness to accept some far-fetched situations. Creators should lay out clear guidelines for the utilization of innovation or wizardry inside the world and comply with these principles all through the account.

An answer for this challenge includes making an innovation or wizardry framework book of scriptures. This report frames the principles, restrictions, and utilizations of the advancements or enchanted components present on the planet. Reliably referring to this guide guarantees that the utilization of innovation lines up with the laid out system, forestalling intelligent irregularities or abrupt headways that might think twice about account cognizance.

The test of keeping up with consistency in ecological subtleties includes guaranteeing that the topography, environment, and biological systems of the made up world stay lucid. Irregularities in these ecological perspectives can prompt an absence of trustworthiness and upset the vivid experience for perusers. Creators should lay out an itemized comprehension of the topography and environment of their reality and apply this information reliably.

An answer for this challenge is the production of an extensive natural aide. This guide ought to detail the geology, environment zones, verdure, and fauna of the imaginary world. Routinely counseling this aide during the creative cycle guarantees that natural depictions line up with the laid out geology, making a more striking and steady depiction of the world.

Guaranteeing variety and portrayal in the made up world is a test that creators should address to make comprehensive and credible stories. Neglecting to address different points of view, societies, and characters can prompt a restricted and homogeneous world. Creators should effectively consolidate variety in their reality building, taking into account different social foundations, nationalities, sexual orientations, and encounters.

An answer for this challenge includes a cognizant work to remember different points of view for the production of the made up world. Creators ought to effectively research and draw motivation from various societies, guaranteeing that the world mirrors the wealth of genuine variety. Awareness perusers from assorted foundations can give significant input, assisting creators with keeping away from generalizations and depict characters truly.

Beating the test of keeping up with peruser commitment all through the world-building process requires a sensitive harmony among detail and pacing. An excess of detail can overpower perusers, while too little can bring about an absence of interest in the made up universe. Creators should check the degree of detail expected for every part of the world and decisively reveal data to keep up with interest and interest.

In the tremendous region of the universe, where systems spin like vast artists, and stars shine like far off fireflies, there exists an embroidery of interconnected universes and domains. This inestimable ensemble winds around together the texture of presence, making a congruity that resounds across the endless spans of existence. Inside this divine mosaic, endless human advancements rise and fall, each contributing its interesting song to the fabulous organization of the universe.

At the core of this enormous expressive dance lies the World Produce, a heavenly pot where the principal components of the truth are formed and shaped. It is here that the grandiose designers, creatures of incomprehensible power and astuteness, make the actual substance of presence. From the early stage energies of the Manufacture, universes are conceived, each with own arrangement of regulations and standards administer the recurring pattern of life.

One such world is Eldoria, a domain washed in the delicate gleam of a double sun framework. Its scenes are essentially as different as the shades of a painter's range, going from the translucent timberlands of Luminescia to the searing deserts of Embera. Eldoria is a universe of sorcery, where hidden energies move through the actual veins of the land, and legendary animals meander openly.

In the drifting city of Aetheria, based after suspending islands suspended overhead, the occupants tackle the force of the Aether to fuel their high level development. Aircrafts float through the mists, impelled by the very embodiment that gives life to Eldoria. The Aetherians, with their shining wings and iridescent eyes, are sensitive to the enchanted flows that course through the sky.

Underneath the outer layer of Eldoria lies the underground domain of Emberdeep, a complex organization of caves enlightened by the bioluminescent gleam of verdure that flourishes without daylight. Here, the Emberfolk, a race of creatures with liquid centers, fashion their homes from the residing rock and outfit the geothermal energies that heartbeat through the earth.

Be that as it may, Eldoria is certainly not a detached diamond in the enormous span. It is nevertheless one of the heap universes that populate the embroidery of creation. Across the star-tossed voids, there exists an organization of heavenly passages known as the Astral Juncture. These enchanted entries associate unique domains, taking into consideration the trading of information, culture, and exchange among the horde civic establishments that speck the enormous scene.

One such domain connected to Eldoria is Astralis, a domain of ethereal excellence and translucent scenes. The Astralites, creatures of unadulterated light and energy, cross the brilliant extensions that range the tremendous breadths between drifting islands. Their general public is based upon the quest for information and illumination, with transcending libraries containing the aggregated insight of ages.

As Eldoria flourishes, so too does the fragile equilibrium of the universe. The divine energies that course through the World Produce are not without their gatekeepers. The Infinite Managers, antiquated creatures of colossal power, look after the embroidery of presence, guaranteeing that the strings of reality remain unfrayed. Their fortification, roosted on the edge of the universe, fills in as a nexus of enormous energies and a stronghold against the infringing powers of disorder.

However, even in the agreeable dance of the universe, conflicting notes can arise. Past the span of the Astral Juncture, in the shadowed corners of the grandiose embroidery, a noxious power blends. The Voidborn, elements brought into the world of the vacancy between universes, look to unwind the strings of creation and dive the universe into everlasting haziness.

The Voidborn's ringlets arrive at across the Astral Conjunction, trying to ruin the heavenly passages and bend the actual texture of the real world. Murmurs of their malignance reverberation through the infinite breezes, and the occupants of Eldoria feel the quakes of an approaching tempest.

In Aetheria, researchers pore over old books, looking for signs to the idea of the looming danger. In Emberdeep, the Emberfolk brace their underground urban communities, directing the geothermal energies to make guarded wards against the infringing dimness.

As the enormous strain mounts, a prediction rises up out of the records of the Astralites. A particularly favored one, a divine guide, will get up against the infringing void and reestablish harmony to the universe. This particularly favored one, directed by the murmurs of the Grandiose Managers, will leave on an excursion that rises above the limits of universes and aspects.

In the core of Eldoria, an apparently standard individual finds idle powers arousing inside. Moved by the enormous energies that course through the world, this far-fetched legend starts to hear the weak reverberations of the Divine Tune, the agreeable song that ties the universe together. Directed by a supernatural instinct, the legend goes ahead on a journey to unwind the secrets of their newly discovered capacities and to face the approaching haziness that takes steps to inundate the domains.

The excursion takes the legend across the assorted scenes of Eldoria, from the transcending towers of Aetheria to the twisted profundities of Emberdeep. En route, the legend experiences a partnership of different partners, each having novel abilities and viewpoints. Together, they structure their very own embroidery, a mosaic of solidarity and solidarity that reflects the inestimable dance unfurling on a more stupendous scale.

As the legend dives further into the privileged insights of the universe, they open the genuine capability of their heavenly capacities. The Aether turns into a conductor for inconceivable accomplishments of flight and control of energy, while the geothermal energies of Emberdeep engage the legend with the strength of the living earth. The Astral Intersection itself turns into a nexus of force, permitting the legend to navigate among domains and gather information from the people of old.

The vast embroidery starts to move as the legend's process unfurls. The Astral Intersection responds to their presence, reverberating with the harmonies of the Heavenly Tune. The Infinite Managers, seeing from their fortress, perceive the development of another power, an offset to the infringing void. The legend's journey becomes interwoven with the actual destiny of the universe, and the strings of their predetermination mesh into the astronomical texture.

However, the Voidborn are not inactive. They send forward their messengers, shadowy creatures that try to snuff out the heavenly light that the legend addresses. The grandiose breezes yell with their malignant murmurs, and the legend faces preliminaries that test their solidarity as well as their purpose. Treacheries and penances mark the legend's excursion, each a powerful note in the stupendous orchestra of their fate.

In the divine observatory of Aetheria, the researchers unravel the antiquated predictions and uncover the real essence of the Voidborn. Brought into the world from the grandiose void, these substances look to consume the actual embodiment of presence, abandoning a barren vacancy. The Astral Conjunction, when a reference point of solidarity, presently wavers near the very edge of debasement, its doors undermined by the infringing shadows.

The legend's cooperation, limited by the common perspective of safeguarding the astronomical agreement, wanders into the core of the Astral Juncture. There, in the midst of the twirling energies of the heavenly entryways, they stand up to the Voidborn in a climactic fight that resonates across the domains. The vast energies conflict, and the actual texture of reality shivers with the power of the battle.

Amidst the disorder, the legend takes advantage of the center of their heavenly capacities, diverting the joined energies of Aether, Ash, and the Astral Intersection. The Heavenly Melody arrives at a crescendo, muffling the grating murmurs of the Voidborn. The legend turns into a living course of inestimable power, a vessel through which the congruity of the universe streams.

The fight arrives at its pinnacle as the legend faces the exemplification of the Voidborn, a whirling frenzy of murkiness and vacancy. The legend's partners, each contributing their novel assets, stand joined against the infringing void. The Heavenly Tune, presently a strong song of praise, reverberates through the Astral Conversion, cleansing the defilement and reestablishing harmony to the inestimable embroidery.

As the last reverberates of the fight disappear, the legend remains in the midst of the grandiose energies, their structure rising above the limits of the human.

The Astronomical Guardians, their fortress aglow with heavenly light, recognize the legend's victory. The Astral Conjunction, once compromised by obscurity, presently transmits with reestablished splendor, and the domains associated by its scaffolds prosper in the consequence of the grandiose clash.

The legend's excursion, set apart by hardships, has not just saved Eldoria from the grip of the Voidborn however has additionally reaffirmed the fragile equilibrium of the universe. The assorted civilizations across the domains, when separated by the boundlessness of room, presently settle on something worth agreeing on in the common triumph over the powers of tumult. The Astral Conjunction, a demonstration of the interconnectedness of universes, turns into an image of solidarity and collaboration.

The legend, presently an extraordinary being of inestimable embodiment, decides to turn into a gatekeeper of the Astral Conjunction. Their presence guarantees that the vast woven artwork stays undisturbed, and the Divine Melody keeps on resounding across the domains. The cooperation, fashioned in the cauldron of astronomical struggle, spreads to their particular countries, conveying with them the illustrations gained from the legend's excursion.

Eldoria, washed in the double suns' delicate gleam, enters another time of success and collaboration. The Aetherians, Emberfolk, and Astralites, when disconnected by the boundlessness of room, presently take part in social trades and exchange worked with by the renewed Astral Conversion. The enormous congruity, once undermined by friction, presently flourishes as a demonstration of the strength of presence.

www.ingramcontent.com/pod-product-compliance
Lightning Source LLC
LaVergne TN
LVHW010222070526
838199LV00062B/4684